~~3.95~~

£3.00
6/3/24

P-51 MUSTANG

Bison Books

P-51 MUSTANG

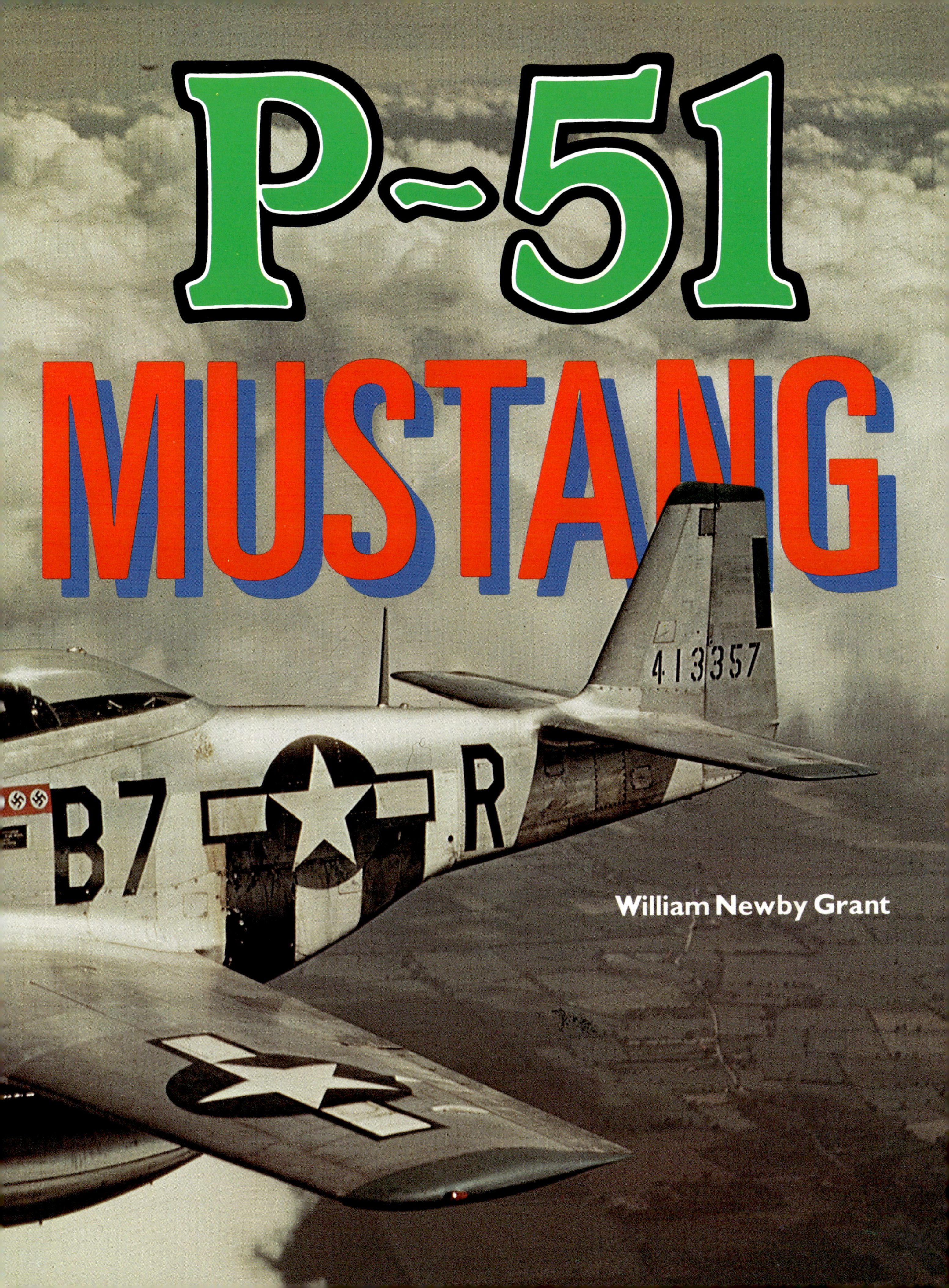

William Newby Grant

First published in 1981 by
Bison Books Ltd.
176 Old Brompton Road
London SW5
England

ISBN 0 86124 135 5

Printed in Hong Kong

Reprinted 1985

Page 1: **Air-to-air view of a P-51B from the 354th Fighter Squadron of the 335th Fighter Group, 8th Air Force fitted with a Malcolm canopy.**
Page 2-3: **Lieutenant Vernon Richards flying his P-51D of the 374th Fighter Squadron, 361st Fighter Group of the 8th Air Force.**
Page 4-5: **Prototype Cavalier Mustang II - a postwar COIN development.**

CONTENTS

INTRODUCTION

The North American P-51 Mustang fighter which flew with the United States Army Air Force and the Royal Air Force during World War II epitomizes American drive and initiative in its conception and design, while its performance was greatly enhanced in later models by the fitting of the British Rolls-Royce Merlin engine. Its story is one of success; from unpromising beginnings, the Mustang went on to become the high-altitude long-range escort fighter *par excellence* once the Merlin was installed. Before this it mainly flew low-level reconnaissance missions for which it proved eminently suitable. However with long-range tanks, the Merlin Mustangs could reach beyond Berlin and range over Europe as far as Austria and Czechoslovakia from the United Kingdom.

During the war it was employed as a fighter, fighter-bomber, dive bomber and reconnaissance aircraft. The basic design was so sound that the only modifications, apart from the engine, were concerned with increasing its armament, its range, and its pilot's all-round vision.

From airfields and landing grounds along the east coast of Britain, in Italy, France, Burma, China and the Pacific, the P-51 carried the war to the enemy and from 1944 played a large part in dominating the skies over Germany. Between 1 July

P-51D of the 376th Fighter Squadron, 361st Fighter Group based at Little Walden wearing invasion stripes.

1940 and 31 August 1945 a total of 14,501 P-51s of all Marks were produced, and the original stipulated cost per machine of $50,000 was only exceeded by $500. By way of comparison a Republic P-47 Thunderbolt cost $83,000 and a Boeing B-17 Flying Fortress $187,742.

The P-51 was a fine airplane. Most pilots who flew the early Allison-engined aircraft preferred them to the later Merlin-powered ones which were harder to handle. The Mustang was on balance the equal of all piston-engined opponents which it encountered, and also had the pleasing lines which so often herald a machine with performance to match. It was maneuverable, carried a respectable armament and because of its weight was fast in the dive. While the P-51 must be placed in context with all the other participants of the war in the air, it is fair to say that it made an inestimable contribution to ultimate Allied victory. The narrative which follows unfolds its development and traces its participation in the battles of World War II and Korea, where the Mustang also played an important part, as well as touching on the more peaceful but no less hectic uses to which it was put in peacetime.

William Newby Grant

CONCEPTION AND EA

When the British Purchasing Commission led by Sir Henry Self was sent to the United States in 1938 with the aim of acquiring American-built military aircraft which the Government realized would soon be needed, it visited a number of major aircraft manufacturing companies. At the time America was pursuing a policy of strict neutrality but nevertheless, during the years of depression in the 1930s, its aircraft manufacturers were delighted to receive orders to build warplanes of various types. Providing the purchasing power was not actually at war this was acceptable to Congress. The Royal Air Force promptly benefited from the purchase of the Lockheed Hudson – based on the Company's Model 14 Electra airliner – and the AT–6 Harvard which was manufactured by North American Aviation Inc.

North American Aviation typified American drive, energy and enthusiasm and, as a result of the Harvard contract, took its place among the front rank American aviation companies. It had arrived on the scene comparatively late in 1928, and since 1934 had devoted its attention to building military airplanes. It was a California-based company, located at the Los Angeles Municipal Airport (or Mines Field) at Inglewood.

In 1939 the United States placed an embargo on the export of military equipment, but an act passed by Congress permitted the shipment of this in the purchasing power's own merchant vessels. As a result the British and the French, who were equally interested in ordering military aircraft for the Armée de l'Air, were still able to acquire them. The decision to allow the exporting to continue reflects the fundamental American good will toward the two nations. It also made sound business sense, enabling the American aircraft industry to gear itself up to mass-production methods. This was of considerable importance to the United States after the Japanese attack on Pearl Harbor brought her into the war in December 1941.

The president of North American Aviation was James H Kindelberger. 'Dutch' Kindelberger had amassed a wealth of manufacturing experience with the Glenn Martin and Douglas Companies before joining North American Aviation. He had also toured Germany and Great Britain to visit their respective aircraft factories in the late 1930s. His vice-president was John Atwood who had been chief engineer of the company, a post now filled by Raymond Rice. North American had been both efficient and punctual with its deliveries of AT-6 Harvards to Great Britain, and it was natural that the British

Below: **Curtiss P-40 Hawk. The British Purchasing Commission were so impressed by the Hawk's performance that they commissioned North American to produce an improved P-40 – the P-51.**

RLY HISTORY

Purchasing Commission should approach it with a view to producing the Curtiss P-40 Hawk (which was to become the RAF's Tomahawk 1), a type for which orders had been placed in 1940 by the British and the French. The Curtiss Hawk utilized the Allison in-line engine and proved to be a machine of versatility and strength, particularly suited to Army co-operation and low-level attack operations. However it was not supercharged, and this meant its performance at altitude was mediocre. The Purchasing Commission was well aware of its limitations, but *faute de mieux* pressed ahead with orders which amounted to a total of 1740, shared between the RAF and the Armée de l'Air.

To the board of North American Aviation it appeared that, however worthy an airplane the P-40 might be, a better machine could be designed. When the proposition to build the P-40 was put to the company in January 1940, James Kindelberger and John Atwood approached the British Purchasing Commission with the suggestion that North American design a fighter of their own. They saw Colonel William Cave and Air Commodore G B A Baker of the Commission at their New York offices and discussed the proposal. It was evidently well received since in April, Atwood was summoned to Sir Henry Self who, after studying P-40 wind-tunnel test reports furnished by John Atwood, signed a draft contract for 320 NA-73 fighter aircraft – as the projected machine's designation was to be. The aircraft would incorporate the Allison engine of the P-40 in a revolutionary low-drag airframe capable of mass production and armed to British specifications.

Time was of the essence in the spring of 1940 and Sir Henry Self's decision was a daring one. Despite their proven efficiency in Harvard deliveries the North American Company had no experience of building fighter aircraft, so the ordering of 320 machines of a type not yet even designed was a singular act of faith.

Frantic activity now took place at the company. On 24 April 1940 the engineers at Inglewood were notified by telegram and immediately commenced drawings, for only outline sketches had been available for Sir Henry Self's perusal. Plans were made overnight by Edgar Schmued, Chief Designer of the company, in collaboration with Raymond Rice and sent direct to John Atwood in New York. There he presented them to the members of the Commission who confirmed the order for the 320 machines on 29 May 1940.

1. F-51D of the Dominican Republic postwar.
2. Curtiss P-40 Hawk.
3. A P-51D
4. Colonel Donald Blakeslee in the cockpit of his P-51.

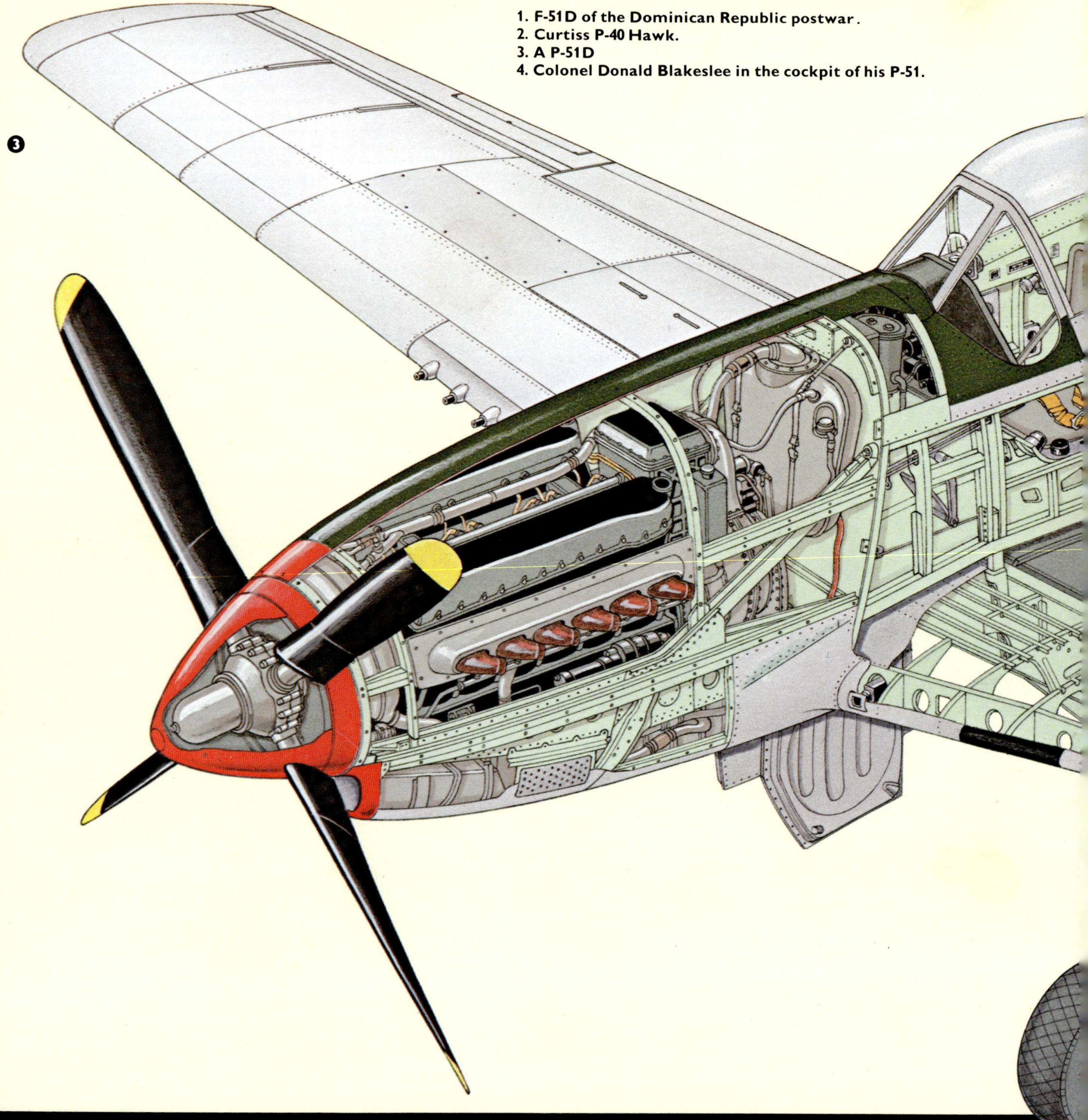

4

6
COOLANT
FULL

7

5

4
DJIGOOBLIE II

1. P-51D of the 504th Fighter Squadron, 339th Fighter Group based at Fowlmere, Cambridgeshire.
2. The fourth production XP-51 (serial 41-38) tested by the USAAF.
3. A P-51D, an earlier version with six .5 caliber machine guns.
4. Staff Sergeants James Lammering and Wilbur Stewart working on a P-51.
5. 108 US-gallon auxiliary fuel tank is fitted beneath a P-51.
6. Control column and cockpit detail.
7. Cockpit controls:
 1 cockpit floodlight
 2 gunsight
 3 cockpit floodlight
 4 cockpit floodlight
 5 throttle
 6 compass
 7 clock
 8 suction gauge
 9 manifold pressure gauge
 10 remote control
 11 altimeter
 12 directional gyro
 13 flight indicator
 14 RPM counter
 15 oxygen flow blinker indicator
 16 mixture lever
 17 propeller control
 18 carburetor mixture control
 19 undercarriage position indicator
 20 air speed indicator
 21 turn and bank indicator
 22 rate of climb indicator
 23 coolant temperature gauge
 24 oil temperature and fuel and oil gauges
 25 oxygen economizer
 26 cockpit cover jettison handle
 27 cockpit floodlight switch
 28 control column
 29 gun and bomb switches
 30 parking brake
 31 instructions for parking brake
 32 engine primer
 33 oxygen pressure gauge
 34 oxygen system warning light
 35 bomb lever
 36 undercarriage selector
 37 booster pump switches
 38 supercharger control
 39 warning light for supercharger
 40 starter
 41 oil dilution switch
 42 ignition switch
 43 compass light switch
 44 gunsight lamp switch
 45 cockpit floodlight switch
 46 fuel cock and tank selector
 47 hydraulic pressure gauge
 48 fairing door emergency control

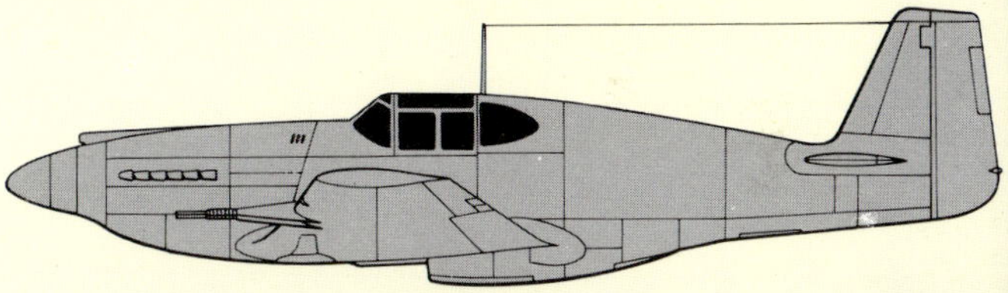

P-51 Mustang 1A

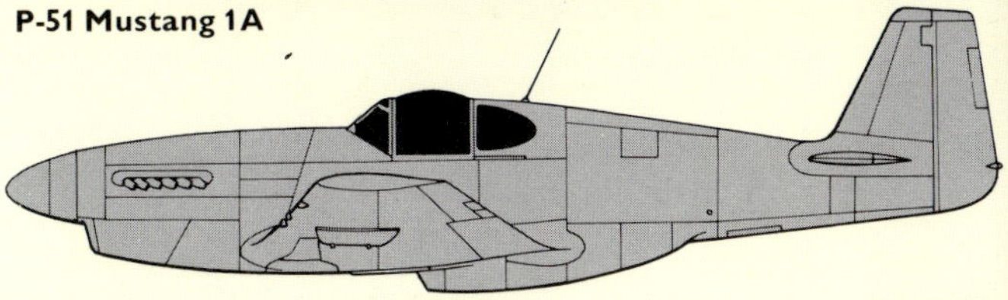

P-51B Mustang III

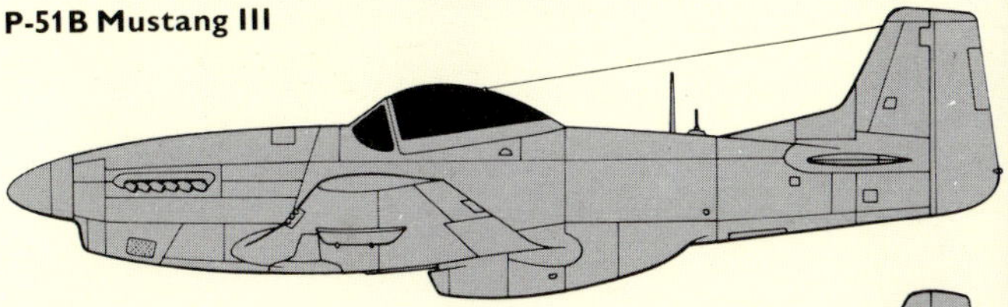

P-51D

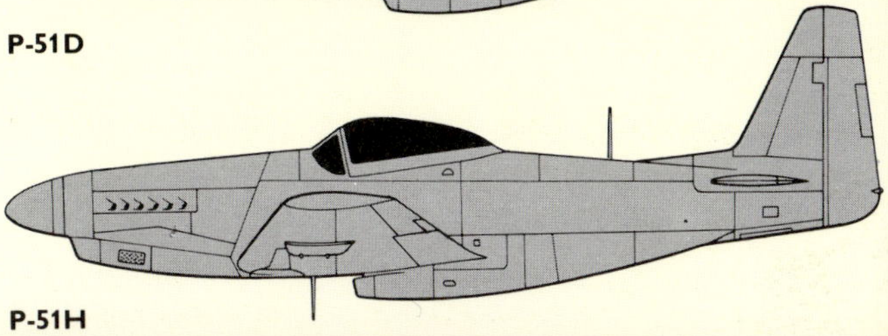

P-51H

Stipulations accompanied the order, however. The NA-73 prototype was to be ready in the time it would have taken North American to tool up for P-40 production, namely 120 days, and the cost per aircraft was not to exceed $50,000. Of these the time scale was critical, and the company set to at once. The Allison V-1710 power plant was to be housed in a low-drag airframe and from the start strenuous efforts were made to reduce drag in every conceivable way. The fuselage was as thin as practicable, with the Allison mounted in a close-fitting cowling. Its radiator was installed below the fuselage slightly to the rear of the cockpit, and there was a small carburetor air intake above the nose. To reduce the unavoidable drag of the radiator duct this was aerodynamically designed, and a certain amount of additional thrust was even provided by a variable exit shutter. Such attention to detail was to be fully rewarded.

An innovation in fighter airplane design was the laminar flow airfoil section wing. This was an advanced concept only recently pioneered and designed by the National Advisory Committee for Aeronautics at North American Aviation. It consisted of a section in which the maximum chord thickness was well aft of the conventional position near the leading edge. The laminar flow was thereby maintained longer before it began to create turbulence, and by maintaining the boundary layer was instrumental in reducing drag. The original NA-73 was not intended to have this wing, and its adoption was the result of Ed Horkey and his team of aerodynamicists' studies. Initial wind-tunnel tests held at the California Institute of Technology on a one-quarter-scale wing proved disappointing, however; the wing's behavior in the stall appeared unsatisfactory, and minor alterations had little effect. This was a severe setback for the design team, but tests conducted in a larger wind-tunnel at the University of Seattle, Washington, proved that the previous results had been misleading, and that the wingtip turbulence problems previously indicated had now disappeared.

These tests also highlighted the drag induced by the unavoidably large radiator duct needed for cooling the glycol for the liquid-cooled Allison. Laminar flow problems associated with the boundary layer in front of it appeared to result in air not being reduced in velocity as it entered the radiator as planned, without which the projected ram effect to help counteract drag could not take place. The slight lowering of the front of the duct solved this problem, and the air slowed down and expanded to draw heat from the radiator before being ejected.

Everyone at North American was working to maximum capacity. Each department constantly checked findings and mockups were made of all assemblies. The NA-73 had to be suitable for mass-production methods, and so castings were employed. The 120-day deadline was achieved. Indeed the prototype NA-73X was wheeled out on 30 August 1940 with three days to spare. The machine lacked an engine, and rested upon AT-6 wheels, but at least it was an airplane of clean lines which had taken a mere 117 days from conception to birth. Allisons had suffered production delays with the 1550hp V-1710-F3R engine and it was October before engine and airframe could be married, but during this period it was apparent to the Purchasing Commission that the design was sound, and a further 300 machines were ordered.

On 26 October 1940 the prototype NA-73X, registration number NX 19998, with chief test pilot Vance Breeze at the controls lifted off Mines Field. The twenty-minute flight which

Left: **P-51B undergoing repair at Repair and Maintenance Centre, Warton, Lancs.**

followed was the realization of a highly ambitious project and a triumph for the North American company. The pilot's report was satisfactory, and the only problems which manifested themselves during the first four flights were minor overheating ones. Unfortunately the fifth flight on 20 November ended in disaster with the aircraft lying on its back beyond the airfield's perimeter. The test pilot, Paul Balfour, escaped unhurt. An error in switching fuel tanks had resulted in fuel starvation. In the inevitable forced landing which followed the machine struck soft ground and overturned.

This was naturally enough a severe blow to the company, but sufficient had already been learned about the NA-73 to realize that it was a success, and production could begin on the 620 machines which the British had ordered. At this time it acquired the name of Mustang; the British have always preferred names to designations and that of the wild horse of the southern states seemed a suitable choice, as it combined power and American ancestry.

The Mustang Mark I supplied to the Royal Air Force was provided under the terms of the Lend-Lease Bill which became law in March 1941. By that time British dollar reserves were seriously depleted and President Franklin D Roosevelt, intent on maintaining the flow of supplies to beleaguered Great Britain, had inaugurated the Bill as a gesture of solidarity as well as of unparalleled generosity. Considering Great Britain's survival 'vital to the defense of the United States' he authorized supplies to continue, and the second production Mustang, serial AG 346, was shipped to the United Kingdom in October 1941 to arrive at Liverpool on the 24th. During the Atlantic crossing the convoy with which it travelled was subjected to air attack, but it arrived safely, was assembled at Speke and test flown in November. The first Mustang produced, AG 345, remained in the United States for flight development testing.

Below: **AG 345 – the first production Mustang for the RAF was retained for testing in the USA after its first flight which took place on 16 April 1941.**

In construction the Mustang was a low-wing cantilever monoplane whose laminar flow wing consisted of two sections bolted together at the center line of the fuselage, where the upper surface formed the cockpit floor. The wing, with five-degree dihedral, was a two-spar all-metal structure with an Alclad skin, and the spars had single-plate flanges and extruding top and bottom booms. The finish of the wing was critical to its performance, and had a direct influence upon the aircraft's speed and range. The remainder of the structure consisted of pressed ribs with flanged holes cut to lighten them and extruding lateral stringers. On each side of the center line and between the spars on each wing were self-sealing nonmetallic fuel tanks, with a total capacity of 184 US-gallons, to which access was gained by small hatch covers on the underneath of each wing. The wing's rear spar accommodated the aileron hinges and slotted flaps, which could be lowered to up to fifty degrees in five seconds to enable high rate turns to be made. The pitot head tube was fitted beneath the starboard wing, a landing light was set in its leading edge. The wing area was 233.19sq ft.

The fuselage of the Mustang was oval in shape and consisted of three sections – engine, main and tail. The engine section mounted two V-shaped cantilever engine bearers built up of plate webs, and with top and bottom extruded numbers, each of which was attached at two points to the 6mm-thick fireproof front bulkhead of the main section. The Vee 12-cylinder Allison engine was attached to these bearers, encased in the streamlined engine cowling, whose line was interrupted only by the top-mounted carburetor air intake. A twelve US-gallon oil tank was housed in the engine compartment.

The main fuselage section consisted of two beams, each side beam comprising two longerons which formed the caps, and the skin was reinforced by vertical frames forming the webs. These two longerons continued aft of the cockpit – which was set low into the fuselage to minimize drag and to which access was gained via a small door opening to port, while the canopy hinged to starboard – to a semi-monocoque structure which was reinforced by vertical frames. The rear part of the main

fuselage section extended further aft to form the detachable tail section. For the pilot's protection the front windshield was of 38mm laminated bullet-proof glass, and 8mm and 11mm armor plating was fitted behind his back. A reinforced crash arch offered protection in the event of his machine overturning, and the SCR-695 radio was mounted behind the cockpit.

The cantilever tail assembly consisted of a one-piece tailplane with detachable tips. The tailplane and fin were built up from two spars with extruded stringers and pressed ribs, and were also Alclad-covered. Trim tabs were fitted to the dynamically-balanced control surfaces, and the elevators and rudder were interchangeable.

The main landing gear was retractable, as was the steerable tail wheel. The two cantilever legs with their shock-absorbers were hinged to large forged fittings which, in turn, were bolted to reinforced ribs. When retracted inward by hydraulic pressure the undercarriage assembly lay forward of the main spar and was covered by wheel well covers, and even when the undercarriage was lowered the inner covers closed to improve the air flow. The brakes were also hydraulically operated, and the 11ft 10in wide track undercarriage endowed the aircraft with considerable stability when operating with a heavy load from rough ground.

Until now the Mustang had been designed by Americans for use by the British; initial United States Army Air Force (USAAF) interest was shown when two of the first production batch of ten machines were acquired as XP-51s and sent to the USAAF Test Center at Wright Field, Ohio. In the meantime Mustang Is began to arrive across the Atlantic in convoys and on arrival were assembled at Speke. Of the original 620 ordered, twenty were lost at sea when the merchantmen carrying them were sunk, but a steady stream arrived in 'CKD' condition – Crated Knocked Down – inside 35ft long wooden crates and covered in protective packing and grease. They were already camouflaged in the standard RAF day-fighter color scheme of dark green and dark earth upper surfaces, with sky (duck-egg blue) below, and spinners and an 18in wide fuselage band of the same color.

Above: **Franklin D Roosevelt and Winston Churchill meet at Quebec in August 1943, to discuss the second front in Europe.**

Tests were conducted as soon as possible at the Aeroplane and Armament Experimental Establishment at Boscombe Down on Salisbury Plain. These revealed that the Mustang I was a very sound machine with a useful turn of speed. It was capable of 375mph at 15,000ft, whereas the RAF's Spitfire V achieved some 340mph, but the Spitfire's rate of climb was superior at seven minutes to 20,000ft. The Mustang needed eleven minutes, mainly because of the limitations of the unsupercharged Allison engine at altitude, and partly because the Mustang, at 8600lb was some 1700lb heavier. It immediately became apparent that the V-1710 engine was the Mustang's greatest disadvantage. At 11,800ft it produced 1150hp (1470hp for War Emergency) but above this height performance tailed off considerably, maximum speed dropping to 357mph at 21,000ft, which meant that it was outclassed by both the Spitfire V and the Messerschmitt Bf 109F.

During the 1920s and 1930s the American Aviation industry had largely ignored the liquid-cooled in-line engine, choosing instead to concentrate on the development of the air-cooled radial. The latter was simpler, lighter and of known reliability, and even with the advent of modern low-wing monoplane fighters of the 1930s, designers still tended to retain the radial, despite the drag penalty incurred by the larger frontal area. The state of development of in-line engines was, therefore, not as advanced in the United States as elsewhere.

Various other drawbacks came to light, including the limitations of visibility from the cockpit, and the difficulty of fitting tall pilots into it. There was also the risk of damage from foreign objects when the slipstream from the propeller blasted loose objects into the mouth of the radiator duct when taxying over rough ground. These were, however, offset by the findings of the pilots engaged in the evaluation of the Mustang. At low altitudes it handled beautifully, was responsive, stable, maneuverable and fast in the dive. Initial skepticism from the RAF about American claims on the latter was dispelled when a speed of 500mph was attained and the Allison engine ran sweetly.

The question now arose as to how the airplane might best be employed. Its poor performance at altitude clearly indicated that it would not survive when matched against the latest Messerschmitt 109 fighters, and by the winter of 1940, with the Battle of Britain won, Fighter Command was intent on developing the Spitfire for high-altitude work. The lower the Mustang flew the happier it seemed, so the logical place for it was with Army Co-operation Command. This Command's objective was to provide close support for the Army, acquire intelligence for it by means of aerial photography and fly tactical reconnaissance missions. The Mustang was admirably suited to this work.

ALLISON-ENGINED MU

A change in philosophy took place in the Royal Air Force's Army Co-operation Command following experience gained in France in 1940. It was clear that only fast moving, highly maneuverable aircraft would stand a reasonable chance of survival in low-level photographic reconnaissance missions. The Mustang Is of Army Co-operation Squadrons were fitted with F.24 cameras which were mounted behind the pilot's seat to point out to port through a clear-vision panel, and which could take films of either 125 or 250 exposures to produce prints 5in by 5in. Camera alignment was by means of a mark on the trailing edge of the port wing, and this required both nicety of judgment and a cool head when flying against defended targets. Operational height was around 900ft and Mustangs flew in pairs; the leader took the photographs while his wingman provided top cover.

The Mustang was a welcome replacement for the aircraft which it had eclipsed, the Curtiss P-40 Tomahawk which had been employed until 1942 on Army Co-operation duties. In January that year the first Mustang had been collected by the first of eighteen planned Mustang Squadrons. By April 1942 26 Squadron, based at Gatwick Airfield south of London, was equipped but not operational, as were 2, 238, 400 and 414 Squadrons of the RAF's 39 Wing. The 400 (City of Toronto) and 414 (Sarnia Imperials) Squadrons were from the Royal Canadian Air Force. The Mustang was capable of considerably more than merely taking photographs; its low-level operating height meant that opportunity targets which presented themselves could be engaged using the aircraft's armament. This consisted of two .5in Browning machine guns with 400 rounds of ammunition, each mounted inside the Allison's engine compartment, synchronized to fire through the propeller arc and with blast tubes emerging beneath the nose. In each wing a further .5in with two .3in machine guns were housed, thus bringing the total of guns to eight. For the .5in guns a variety of ammunition was available. The M2 Ball Cartridge fired a 700 grain bullet at 2810ft per second, and Armor Piercing M2, Tracer M10, Incendiary M1 and AP/Incendiary rounds were also used. The rate of fire per barrel was 800 rounds per minute.

On 10 May 1942 the Mustang I flew its first operational sortie against the French coast in the area of Berck-sur-Mer. It was AG 418, flown by Flying Officer G Dawson of 26 Squadron based at Gatwick. This was the first of many such forays – known as Populars – during the course of which Mustangs engaged many targets of opportunity and encountered the highly accurate German light anti-aircraft defenses which were to exact such a toll of them. These defenses and the very nature of low-level high-speed flying combined to make such reconnaissance missions extremely dangerous; the first Mustang to be lost was AG 415, flown by Pilot Officer H Taylor, which crashed into the water while strafing a barge in mid-July. On 24 July a press day was held at Sawbridgeworth.

RAF Army Co-operation Command Mustang Is of 2 Squadron, Sawbridgeworth.

STANGS

Mustangs from all five Squadrons flew in support of the ill-fated amphibious assault on Dieppe on 19 August 1942. A total of 72 sorties were flown and nine aircraft were lost and two further ones were written off. The British losses were only partly offset by the destruction of one enemy aircraft – a Focke Wulf FW 190 – which fell to the guns of a 414 (Canadian) Squadron Mustang flown by Flying Officer Hollis Hills, an American volunteer flying with the RCAF. Despite the losses, Mustangs continued to harass the enemy along the Channel coast and inland areas, and maintained the task of keeping up-to-date photographic intelligence of German defenses. Other tasks allotted included flying sorties to identify shipping and intercepting low-level attacks by Focke-Wulf 190s along the British south coast. Over Europe any train spotted was attacked, as were enemy transport columns and trainer aircraft, and the constant surprise attacks in rear areas must have been most unsettling for the Germans. At the same time it provided evidence to the populations of the occupied countries that the Allies were again on the offensive.

In October 1942 a new type of operation was authorized. This was known as the Rhubarb, and made use of bad weather and low cloud to provide suitable conditions for engaging specific targets on the Continent. For these missions Army Co-operation Command Mustangs flew under the operational control of Fighter Command, and targets included enemy airdromes, transport of all types and any aircraft encountered. A long-range operation took Mustangs into German airspace for the first time on 21 October on a mission to the Dortmund–Ems canal which also incorporated shipping strikes in the Netherlands on the return flight. These Rhubarbs placed an additional strain on the pilots, who now had to contend with poor weather conditions as well as the usual hazards, demands of pilot navigation at low level and the transcription of intelligence data onto special knee pads.

At this time Mustangs carried, in addition to the Sky identification bands around their rear fuselages and spinners, a narrow yellow band painted just inboard of the roundels on the wings. These were introduced to help prevent misidentification of the aircraft by friendly air and ground forces, and were conceived after several Mustangs had been shot down by Allied fighters whose pilots had mistaken the then unfamiliar shape for that of the German Messerschmitt Bf 109 – an understandable mistake since the 109E had square wing tips too. The general outline was also similar, and in any case in air fighting the pilot had to decide whether to open or hold fire in a matter of seconds. The bands tended to compromise the green and gray camouflage pattern and, with the improvements in recognition, were removed before long. The early color scheme had been changed in August 1941 to dark green and ocean gray upper and sea-gray medium lower surfaces. This color scheme was more suited to the cross-Channel operations in which the aircraft were increasingly taking part. At the same time new roundels were introduced and the white part of the fin flash was considerably reduced.

The radius of action of 300 miles was unique for a single-engined fighter and resulted from its clean lines and laminar flow wing. This radius included a generous margin for safety's sake, and took into account transit and operational heights and speeds. It was twice that of Hurricanes and Spitfires and, in an attempt to show the high standard a Mustang was capable of achieving, an enterprising Flight Lieutenant named J Lewkowicz of 309 Czerwienskiej (Polish) Squadron made an unauthorized flight from his base at Dalcross near Inverness in Scotland to Stavanger in Norway and back again on 27 September. Over Stavanger he indulged in a little strafing, and his feat of calculated risk and first-class navigation brought him a commendation as well as the inevitable reprimand. It had proved that the Mustang could penetrate to far greater distances than had previously been considered possible.

In 1943 the first Ranger missions were undertaken. These were flown by small free-lance groups of Mustangs at low level and at 300mph over occupied Europe and over the Bay of Biscay by 414 (Canadian) Squadron. Losses continued to mount, and not all were attributable to enemy action; a flight of four Mustangs from 2 Squadron lost three airplanes when they encountered sea fog while crossing the English coast in Dorset in May and hit high ground. By this time additional Squadrons had been formed or re-equipped with Mustangs, and the RAF now had at its disposal, in addition to the original five, 4, 13, 16, 63, 116, 168, 225, 239, 241, 268, 309 (Polish), 430 (Canadian) and 613 Squadrons. Among them all, 400 (Canadian) Squadron had enjoyed particular success with the large-scale destruction of enemy trains, and one pilot, Flight Lieutenant D Grant, had claimed thirty. Many enemy aircraft had been shot down by day and by night and worthwhile targets had been regularly attacked.

Squadrons were rotated and when not flying on operations provided the air element for Army exercises. Mustang Squadrons – some now equipped with the Mustang Mark IA with four 20mm cannons in place of the eight machine guns – were attached to individual Army formations and helped to train their troops for the invasion. Army Co-operation Command was incorporated into the Second Tactical Air Force in June 1943. Its Mustangs had done excellent work, and a year previously the *Aeroplane* journal provided the following comment on the type: 'Pilots who fly the Mustang praise it so lavishly that they exhaust their superlatives before they have finished their eulogies.'

While the Mustang was winning its spurs in the skies over Europe, the United States had ordered 150 Mustang IAs with their quadruple 20mm M-2 cannons as P-51-NAs in September 1941, and had, of course, taken delivery of the two original RAF production batch. American interest in the field of air support to ground forces for reconnaissance had been heightened following a study of British experience, and when America entered the war on 7 December 1941 after the Japanese attack on Pearl Harbor, attention was directed toward the two rather neglected XP-51s which had been languishing at Wright Field. Fifty-five of the Mustang IAs ordered for the RAF were repossessed and fitted with two K.24 (American-built British F.24) cameras. These were given the designation F-6A and were originally intended to bear the name Apache; however, the name adopted for the RAF machine stuck. The first F-6As flew tactical reconnaissance missions with two Observation Squadrons (111th and 164th) of the 68th Observation Group in North Africa in March 1943. On their tailplanes they carried the Stars and Stripes.

The P-51A was a fighter version ordered for the United States Army Air Force. In place of the cannon they mounted four .5in Brownings in their wings, and 358 were ordered. The P-51A dispensed with the nose armament and was powered by an Allison V-1780-81 engine which provided 1200hp on takeoff and full power at 20,000ft, a considerable advance upon the original P-51. Pylons were provided for underwing stores, which could be either two 500lb bombs or 75 or 150 US-gallon drop tanks. The RAF received fifty examples of the P-51A as the Mustang Mark II; the only Allison-engined Mustangs used by the Americans in the United Kingdom were P-51As converted to F-6A status and flown by the 107th Tactical Reconnaissance Group in October 1943.

The spring of 1942 had seen another development of the Mustang, the A-36A dive bomber. Studies of other air forces

Above: **In its element–an RAF Mustang flies low and fast. The Mustangs' tactics over Occupied Europe were to fly just above the ground and treetops.**

had indicated that fighter aircraft could be employed in this role, and the Mustang's high speed in the dive was put to good use. The first A-36A flew in September 1942 and incorporated various modifications necessary to strengthen the machine. Hydraulically-operated air brakes which opened above and below the wing slowed the rate of descent in a high-angle dive to some 300mph, and bomb shackles were fitted to a heavier than standard wing. Each wing also housed two .5in machine guns and the ventral radiator air duct was modified. An order for 500 A-36s was placed and the first saw action over Pantelleria in June 1943 with the 27th Bomb Group. In Sicily this was joined by the 86th Bomb Group and targets on the island and on the Italian mainland continued to be attacked in support of ground forces from September. The same month saw the title changed to Fighter Bomber Groups and the reduction of one of the four Squadrons in each. Losses had been moving toward unacceptable levels, however; the A-36A was vulnerable in its low-level pull out, and aircraft were known to disintegrate when the unequal extension of the air brakes led to their being over-stressed. Eventually the A-36s were replaced by P-47 Thunderbolts in early 1944, but not before the 27th FB Group won a Distinguished Unit Citation for its operations during the Salerno landings on 10 September 1943.

A-36s flew aerial resupply missions to American ground forces in Italy and some served with the 111th Tactical Reconnaissance Squadron. The name Invader was bestowed upon the aircraft briefly in 1943, but was subsequently allocated to the Douglas A-26 bomber. The RAF received a single A-36A which became EW 998 and on which bombing trials were carried out.

At this stage it is worth comparing the Allison-engined Mustang with an enemy fighter with which it frequently came into contact, the Focke-Wulf FW 190. During the war comparative trials were held both in Great Britain and the United States to evaluate captured enemy machines with the aim of subsequently exploiting any weaknesses. The results of these trials serve only as a guide, for there was a natural enough prejudice toward and preference for one's own machines, and a skilled pilot in an inferior aircraft would probably be able to defeat a less experienced one in a better machine. In a trials report of August 1942 a captured Focke-Wulf 190A-3 was flown against a Mustang IA of the RAF.

Up to 23,000ft, speeds showed little difference except in the band between 10,000ft and 15,000ft, at which height the Mustang was 10-15mph faster. In both standard and zoom climbs the FW 190 was superior, while in a dive there was little to choose. In terms of maneuverability the FW 190 was superior except in radius of turn, and the Mustang was slower to accelerate. If attacked, the FW 190's best option was to climb, since, unlike the Spitfire with its gravity-fed carburetor which cut off fuel under conditions of negative G, the Mustang could dive in pursuit without having to roll inverted and pull back on the stick. To evade the FW 190, a Mustang's pilot's best bet was to execute a sharp turn, since diving would not help. The trial found that the optimum height for the Mustang IA was between 5000ft and 15,000ft. To some extent the report was outdated at the time it appeared because the FW 190A-4 with its water-methanol injection improved its speed, but P-51 development was not static, and the Merlin-engined P-51B was on its way.

Above left: **Training for war–fighter-bomber releasing its bombs at the AAF Tactical Center, Orlando, Florida.**

Left: **Tactical reconnaissance operations: presortie briefing, England, 5 April 1943.**

MERLIN-ENGINED MUS

The Allison Mustangs had proved beyond doubt that the basic design of the airplane was sound, but the limitations of its engine above 25,000ft were succinctly summarized in the RAF opinion that it was 'a bloody good airplane, only it needs a bit more poke.' Consideration had been given to this problem on both sides of the Atlantic, and in England a test pilot named Ronald Harker flew a Mustang I in April 1942 as part of his job of evaluating Allied and enemy types, at the Air Fighting Development Unit at Duxford in Cambridgeshire. Impressed by its handling, he suggested to Rolls-Royce's Chief Aerodynamic Engineer at Hucknall, W Challier, that the Mustang's performance would be considerably enhanced if a Rolls-Royce Merlin 61 with two-speed two-stage supercharger were fitted. This engine had powered a prototype Spitfire IX in which it had produced 417mph at 28,000ft, and both men realized that the combination of this sort of performance with the aerodynamically efficient airframe of the Mustang would revolutionize its potential. Challier estimated that the combination would result in 441mph at 25,600ft. The American Assistant Air Attaché in London, Lieutenant Colonel Thomas Hitchcock, was greatly excited by the prospect, and via his Ambassador arranged to provide the USAAF's General Henry H 'Hap' Arnold with details, and the recommendations of senior RAF officers, including Air Chief Marshal Sir Trafford Leigh-Mallory. Colonel Hitchcock – who, ironically, was to lose his life while flying a Mustang which disintegrated near Salisbury in April 1944 – was convinced the conversion would work, but General Arnold reserved judgment until practical experience had been gained. After all, the USAAF had the P-38 Lightning and the P-47 Thunderbolt in service and, by this stage in 1942 their limitations had not yet been discovered.

Rolls-Royce began to effect the necessary conversion of four Mustangs designated Mustang Xs at Hucknall in June 1942. These aircraft were directed there from Speke and bore the serials AM 203, AM 208, AL 963 and AL 975. This last was the first conversion and, in place of the proposed Merlin 61, a special Merlin 65 with a two-stage supercharger and Bendix-Stromberg fuel injection was fitted. On 13 October 1942 AL 975G took to the air with Rolls-Royce's Chief Test Pilot Ronald Shepherd at the controls.

The Merlin had been neatly installed in the sleek nose of the Mustang on a new engine mounting. Visually the Merlin Mustang differed from its Allison-engined predecessor by the removal of the latter's carburetor air intake above the nose, and its incorporation with the intake scoop for the supercharger intercooler now located below the nose just aft of the spinner. The propeller on AL 975G was a 10ft 9in diameter four-bladed Rotol, although other conversions were tested with a specially designed 11ft 4in propeller. All four machines were to embody a number of modifications in the quest for optimum performance, including a series of alterations to the intercooler air exit on the fuselage sides between exhaust stubs and cockpit. Speed gradually improved, with 413mph in the full supercharger model being attained in November, and 390mph with medium supercharger. Various minor problems such as undercarriage doors opening in flight were rectified. Most striking to the test pilots was the difference the more powerful engine made to the airplane. To those accustomed

Right: **The clean lines of a Packard Merlin-engined P-51.**
Above right: **The neat installation of the Packard-built Rolls-Royce Merlin.**

TANGS

to the docile handling characteristic of the Allison Mustang, its successor proved a very different proposition. It was more vicious in the stall, less directionally stable – although the fitting of a dorsal strake in front of the fin improved this – and much noisier. By early 1943 the performance was such that it took the Merlin-engined Mustang just over six minutes to climb to 20,000ft as opposed to just over nine in the Mustang I.

The second Mustang to be converted was AM 208, and in this aircraft a speed of 433mph was reached at 22,000ft using full supercharger with 18lb per square-inch boost. The AM 203, the third conversion, carried the larger propeller; trials were carried out on this model to determine how new paint finishes affected performance. In February 1943 it was loaned to the USAAF for evaluation. The AL 963 was used for stability and carburation trials, and a special Merlin 65 with maximum boost pressure of 25lb per square inch and finally a Merlin 66 with a new intercooler was fitted. The AM 121, the first Mustang destined for conversion, had been retained for calibration trials but in turn was also fitted with a Merlin. It was extensively tested by the USAAF at Bovingdon, where it flew in the olive drab color scheme and American markings. Rolls-Royce also later studied the feasibility of fitting a Griffon 61 engine, but this venture never proceeded beyond the design stage.

In the United States development was proceeding, too, with the redesign of the P-51 to accommodate the Packard-built Merlin XX engine, the V-1650-3, which corresponded to the Merlin 61. The first two American conversions bearing the serial numbers 41-37352 and 41-37421 were carried out on two Mustang 1As, built for the RAF, and received the designation XP-51B. The first was flown on 30 November 1942 by test pilot Robert Chilton, and suffered overheating problems. These delayed the next flight until late December but General Arnold, now satisfied with the data supplied to him on British experiences with the Mustang X, recommended that large numbers be built, and the first P-51B production aircraft were delivered in June 1943. By careful design both intercooler radiator and main coolant radiator were incorporated into the same scoop, while beneath the nose only a small aperture was needed for the carburetor air intake. The improvement in performance over the P-51A Allison-engined Mustang was dramatic, and a top speed of 453mph at 28,800ft was attained using 1298hp War Emergency boost and a Hamilton Standard four-bladed constant speed propeller of 11ft 2in diameter with paddle blades. Armament consisted of four or six .5in Brownings with a total of 1260 rounds. The wing shackles could accept two 1000lb bombs or drop tanks of 75 or 150 US-gallon capacity. The P-51B weighed 6840lb empty and, in comparison with the P-51A, developed 1400hp for takeoff, 1530hp at 15,750ft, and 1300hp at 26,500ft, thus improving the P-51 A's horsepower at optimum height by some 300.

The P-51B-NA was manufactured from June 1943 by North American Aviation at their Inglewood plant in Los Angeles, where a total of 1988 was eventually produced. The P-51C-NT was built at Dallas in Texas in a second North American factory which began production in August 1943, and where 1750 were built. There was no difference between the aircraft, and the designation merely indicated from which factory they had come. The RAF received 274 P-51Bs and 636 P-51Cs as Mustang Mark IIIs, and the Americans converted a total of 91 into F-6C reconnaissance aircraft. It was in the P-51B and P-51C that the Fighter Commands of the United States Army Air Forces were to go to war in Europe.

Right: **P-51s nearing completion on the Dallas production line, where a total of 1750 P-51Cs were built.**

USAAF OPERATIONS I

On 20 February 1942 General Henry Arnold, Commanding General of the USAAF, sent Brigadier General Ira C Eaker to the United Kingdom to establish the Headquarters of the United States 8th Air Force. In June its Commander, Major General Carl A Spaatz, arrived with a group of Staff Officers at RAF Hendon, and established his Fighter Headquarters on 18 June at Bushey Park a few miles beyond the suburbs of London, close to RAF Fighter Command's HQ at Bentley Priory. Brigadier General Eaker's aim was to launch a strategic air offensive against Germany using the Boeing B-17 Flying Fortress as his principal weapon. The Fortress had a heavy defensive armament, and initially the theoreticians were of the opinion that box formations could lay down such a heavy defensive fire with the interlocking arcs of their .5in machine guns that they would be immune to fighter attack. At this stage the fighter element of the 8th AF was regarded as a purely tactical arm, and thus the first P-51Bs were assigned to the US 9th Air Force, formed in October 1942 for tactical operations – at first with the Middle East Air Force – in support of the forthcoming invasion of Europe under the command of Major General Lewis H Brereton. The 9th AF's 100th Fighter Wing consisted of three Fighter Groups, the 354th (with 353, 355 and 356th Fighter Squadrons), the 357th (with 362, 363 and 364th Fighter Squadrons), and the 363rd (with 380, 381 and 382nd Fighter Squadrons) and moved to the United Kingdom in September 1943. Each Squadron consisted of sixteen aircraft.

All this was in the future. Air Chief Marshal Arthur Harris of Bomber Command and General Spaatz shared the belief that the war with Germany could be won by strategic bombing. While the two bomber forces shared the common aim of destroying Germany's aircraft-manufacturing and oil-production industries, their operations were conducted independently. From the outset the US 8th AF employed day-bombing techniques while the RAF's Bomber Command operated at night.

General Arnold suggested the establishment of five Pursuit – or Fighter – Groups, two of which would be reserved for UK defense while the other three conducted offensive air operations against the Germans. The first Fighter Group which arrived in June 1942 was equipped with Spitfire Vs, the type which had also been flown by the three Eagle Squadrons (71, 122 and 133) of American volunteers serving with the Royal Air Force. Meanwhile the B-17 Bombardment Groups had been formed and began to launch their first unescorted raids against targets in France. The first was an attack on Rouen on 17 August 1942 when twelve B-17s of 97th Bombardment Group accompanied by General Eaker encountered little resistance. The confidence which these early raids built up was soon to be dispelled.

In September 1942 the Eagle Squadrons were transferred to 8th AF Command, but most pilots were reassigned to the

Right: **Escort for the heavy bombers – a Packard Merlin P-51 in olive drab livery.**
Inset: **Brigadier General Ira C Eaker commander of the 8th AF's bomber command, was later to become C in C of the Mediterranean Air Command.**

I EUROPE

Above: **A 9th Air Force P-51B of the 355th Fighter Squadron, 354th Fighter Group.**
Below: **P-51B – the radio and gunsight are visible.**

12th Air Force in North Africa to fly P-38 Lightnings. In December 1942 8th AF Fighter Command began to receive the Republic P-47 Thunderbolt fighters which equipped the 4th, 56th and 78th Fighter Groups for escort duty with the bomber formations. However their maximum range on internal tanks was a mere 175 miles and this meant that, beyond a given point, the bombers flew on unescorted and faced the German fighters alone. In order to increase this range 200 US-gallon ventral drop tanks were fitted, but these proved unsatisfactory since they leaked and because of pressurization problems did not deliver fuel at heights of over 23,000ft. The first raid on Germany accompanied by P-47s was on 17 April 1943 when Bremen was attacked and sixteen B-17s were lost.

During the spring and summer of 1943 the 8th Air Force doggedly continued to send its bombers against Germany and suffered terrible losses as a result, culminating in the second raid on the German ball-bearing factories at Schweinfurt on 27 September 1943 when, of 291 B-17s dispatched, sixty were shot down, seventeen were severely damaged and 121 more were slightly damaged. During a previous raid on the same target in mid-August 36 aircraft had been lost out of a force of 230 on the same day as 24 were shot down during a simultaneous attack on the Messerschmitt factory at Regensburg.

These losses simply could not be sustained. The P-47 fighter escorts had sufficient range to escort the bombers only as far as Aachen on the second Schweinfurt raid, and 8th AF demands for P-51s with their vastly superior range were only met when the first P-51 Group arrived in the November of 1943. From then on the P-47 and P-51 were increasingly to exchange their roles. The P-51 began to operate as an escort at higher altitudes and the P-47 began to operate at a low level.

The 354th Fighter Group had been raised in the United States, trained on P-39 Airacobras, and arrived at Greenham Common airdrome near Newbury in Berkshire on 3 November 1943. This Pioneer Mustang Group was assigned not to the 8th but to the 9th Air Force, but Major General William Kepner of the former swiftly 'borrowed' them for escort duties. On 11 November the first P-51Bs arrived, much to the surprise of the pilots who had been expecting P-47 Thunderbolts. The 354th FG moved to Boxted near Colchester on the Essex coast to gain experience of the type under the command of Lieutenant Colonel Kenneth R Martin. Pilots checked out there on P-51As borrowed from the 10th and 67th Reconnaissance Groups of the 9th AF, and were reinforced by ex-Eagle Squadron members. No longer would the bombers have to fly alone, and the P-51 began to assume a strategic role.

The 354th FG consisted of three Fighter Squadrons, the 353rd, 355th and 356th, and flew its first operational mission on 1 December 1943, the date by which Colonel Martin had stated the Group would be operational. It was led by Major Donald J M Blakeslee, a highly experienced ex-Eagle Squadron pilot who had been sent to Boxted to fly the Mustang in November. Twenty-four P-51Bs took off from this airfield to carry out an offensive sweep over the Belgian and French coasts. The Group's first escort mission was to Amiens on 5 December, this was followed by raids on Emden and Kiel during which 75 US-gallon drop tanks provided a range of 500 miles. The first enemy aircraft to fall to the Group, a

Above: **P-51D from the 343rd Fighter Squadron, 55th Fighter Group, Wormingford, UK.**
Below: **The prototype P-51D.**

Messerschmitt Bf 110, was shot down by Lieutenant Charles Gumm of 355th FS during a raid on Bremen on 16 December, but on the same day the Commanding Officer of the 353rd FS, Major Owen M Seamen, went down into the icy gray waters of the North Sea after suffering engine failure.

By the New Year eight enemy aircraft had been claimed and eight P-51s had been lost, mainly because of mechanical failures. These were mostly problems associated with high-altitude flying, where windshields became covered in frost in the rarefied air six miles above the earth due to inadequate heating. The Packard-built Merlins suffered coolant leaks, and spark plugs became fouled. This problem was solved by the fitting of British-made ones. Guns iced up but a design weakness also manifested itself. When reports of the .5in Brownings' failure to fire were analyzed, it became clear that, when the aircraft was banked in a tight turn, the G forces applied to the belt feed mechanism retarded the ammunition belt and caused difficulties in feeding. Utilizing the recoil energy of the gun, the belt pull was increased to 70lb or to 80lb when an electric motor was used. This led to an improvement, but the configuration of the gun bays still meant that the Brownings had to be canted. A total of 1260 rounds were carried, and in October a new cartridge combining AP, Incendiary and Tracer was introduced.

In a Christmas message to the 8th and 15th Air Forces on 27 December, General Arnold stated 'Destroy the Enemy Air Force wherever you find them, in the air, on the ground and in the factories.' While their task of escorting bombers improved the crews' morale and chances of survival, the P-51 pilots were under considerable strain. Whereas the B-17s had two pilots and a crew, the P-51 pilot sat alone in his pressurized cockpit watching, navigating, scanning his instruments and oxygen supply, with the prospect of two flights over the North Sea in his single-engined machine with possible battle damage on the return one. To add to his difficulties the old problems of misidentification began to recur. On occasions Mustangs were attacked by Thunderbolts.

When he did engage the two most frequently-encountered German fighters, the P-51B pilot did have the advantage of the results of comparative trials carried out in the United Kingdom between his machine and the Messerschmitt Bf 109G-2 and the Focke-Wulf FW 190. These indicated that the P-51B was 50mph faster at all heights up to 28,000ft, beyond that 70mph faster than the FW 190, and between 30mph and 50mph faster than the Me 109. Rates of climbs were similar for all three aircraft, but the Mustang could outdive both German machines. Its radius of turn was marginally better than the Focke-Wulf's and much better than the Messerschmitt's, but while the former's rate of roll was superior, the latter's was inferior because its wing slots had the disconcerting habit of opening. Nevertheless several German fighter pilots maintain that both the German machines' rates of turn were superior and one, Erich Hartmann, who amassed a total of 352 Allied aircraft shot down in 1400 missions, maintains that he could outpace P-51s in the 109, and also obtain an indicated air speed of 480mph at 12,000ft.

With drop tanks fitted the speed at all heights was reduced by some 40–50mph because of additional weight and drag factors, but aerobatics were still possible and, provided the Mustang could convert height into speed, it could still be used offensively. At this stage the P-51B had a range of 1080 miles using its 170 US-gallon internal tanks, and a maximum range of 2600 miles when carrying two 150 US-gallon drop tanks. With 75 US-gallon ones fitted to the wing shackles, the range became 1800 miles, and with an additional self-sealing 85 US-gallon internal fuel tank mounted in the fuselage behind the pilot, the range became 1350 miles at 10,000ft on internal tanks. Consumption was calculated to be 8.85 air miles per gallon. A most important development at this time was the expendable lightweight 108 US-gallon drop tank built by the British firm of Bowaters from compressed paper, plastic and glue. Its life was limited but long enough for the four hours maximum required, and it could be converted into a weapon; unexpended fuel in the tanks could be ignited by incendiary

Above: **9th Air Force pilots 'chow up' at an advanced landing ground after returning from a bombing mission on Le Bourget, an airport in northern France.**

bullets if the tanks were dropped on enemy targets. Engine life of the Merlin was reckoned to be 200 hours.

By way of comparison the P-47 – designed as a bomber escort – originally carried a total of 305 US-gallons internally, which provided 605 miles at cruising speed. The P-47D with its 150 US-gallon ventral tank provided 850 miles. The -25RE could carry 780 US-gallons which, from March 1944 enabled the aircraft to reach Berlin. The P-47, incidentally, doubled the P-51B's armament.

In January 1944 the 354th Pioneer Mustang Group, still under the operational control of the 9th Air Force, was reinforced by two additional P-51 Groups. The 8th Air Force only gained its own P-51s when it exchanged its 358th (P-47) Fighter Group with the 9th Air Force's 357th (P-51) Fighter Group.

This second Mustang Group began operations from Leiston airfield - also known as Saxmundham – just inland from the Suffolk coast on 11 February 1944 under the command of Lieutenant Colonel James Howard. A former Commanding Officer of the 354th FG, Howard had been awarded the Congressional Medal of Honor on 11 January for attacking, single-handed, a large formation of Messerschmitt 110s which were attacking a B-17 Group he was escorting over Halberstadt. Flying P-51B 43-6315 he disrupted the attack and claimed six probables. The same Fighter Group was to provide the 9th AF's top-scoring fighter pilot, Lieutenant Glenn Eagleston, with 18.5 victories, and the 353rd FS's Captain Don M Beerbower shot down 15.5.

The third Mustang Group, the 363rd, was established at Rivenhall in Essex and became operational on 22 February. Three days later the 4th Fighter Group, commanded by Lieutenant Colonel Donald Blakeslee, converted to the P-51 at Debden, and so in the spring of 1944 several hundred Mustangs regularly ranged over the skies of Germany. The 4th Fighter Group provided some of the most successful American fighter pilots of the war, including Captain Don S Gentile, an ex-133 Eagle Squadron member now flying with the 336th Fighter Squadron. Flying P-51B 43-6913 *Shangri-La* and forming a lethal partnership with his wingman, Captain John T Godfrey, Gentile shot down 21.8 enemy aircraft confirmed and his partner eighteen.

The 4th Fighter Group with its component 334, 335 and 336th Fighter Squadrons flew its first mission while the pilots had less than one hour logged on the type. The 336th FS became dispersed on the first planned raid over Berlin on 3 March 1944 because of bad weather, but Blakeslee's P-51s escorted American bombers over the German capital on the

following day, despite appalling weather conditions. On 6 March the 357th FG shot down twenty German aircraft without loss; already rivalry was building up both between Fighter Squadrons within a Group, and between exponents of the P-51 and the P-47 which, it should be remembered, was engaged in combat missions of equal intensity, as indeed were the P-38 Lightnings.

From mid-February 1944 USAAF Mustangs began to dispense with their olive drab finish and it was discovered that in their base metal finish they flew some 5mph faster because of the reduction of skin friction. Some ground crews applied wax polish to their P-51s to improve speed still further. On 23 March color schemes for individual Squadrons were adopted, and the colored markings were applied to spinners, engine cowlings and fin and rudder. This reflected growing Allied air superiority and the infrequency of German attacks on United Kingdom air bases, where camouflage had previously been advisable for dispersed aircraft.

The 4th Fighter Group shot down its 300th victim on 29 March, and such was the range of the Mustang that strafing forays took place on targets as far away as Munich and Berlin in early April. This was highly dangerous because of the effectiveness of the German flak, and destroying aircraft on the ground was no easy way of acquiring victories. The controversial decision to award a victory for an enemy aircraft destroyed while ground strafing was made at this time. Such was the attrition for the German Jagdverbände that by the end of April the 4th FG had amassed 500 victories. On 13 April Don Gentile had contrived to hit the ground while beating up his base at Debden prior to returning to the United States having completed his tour. The tempo increased with the build up to D-Day on 6 June 1944, and over a thousand American fighters were in the air over occupied Europe on a single day late in May.

To follow the fortunes of the 354th Pioneer Mustang Group, on 1 March Lieutenant Gumm suffered engine failure on take off from Boxted in 43-12410 and was killed in the ensuing forced landing. On 17 April the Group moved to a new base at Lashenden in Kent under the command of Lieutenant Colonel George R Bickell, and was awarded a Distinguished Unit Citation. Following the invasion, it flew to France and in July the Supreme Allied Commander, General Dwight D Eisenhower, flew over the battlefield in a Squadron two-seater conversion 43-6877. Shortly after receiving a second Distinguished Unit Citation for destroying 51 enemy aircraft on 25 August, the 354th was ordered to convert on to P-47s. It voiced its displeasure so strongly that in February 1945 it received P-51s back. When the war ended the 354th was the highest scoring USAAF Fighter Group with 701 aerial and 255 ground victories.

The Royal Air Force had, meanwhile, received P-51Bs as the Mustang III, and one Wing operated them from Gravesend in Kent. This was 122 Wing, and consisted of three Squadrons, 19, 65 and 122. Partly because tall pilots found themselves cramped beneath their canopies and partly to improve rearward vision, a bulged canopy similar to the Spitfire's was designed by R Malcolm, and fitted at the A and AEE Boscombe Down. This became known as the Malcolm hood and alleviated the problem which was only solved by the introduction of the full blister canopy on the P-51D. In February 1944 the RAF received its first Malcolm-hooded Mustangs, and the USAAF began a program of modification for its P-51Bs and Cs.

A new Mark of P-51 arrived in the United Kingdom at the time of the invasion, the P-51D. The first Inglewood-built models began to leave the production lines in February 1944 and Dallas-made ones in July. In addition to the blister canopy with its five-ply armored Lucite front panel, other modifications included the lowering of the fuselage top necessitated by the new canopy. This naturally resulted in a reduction of fuselage side area, and a strake was fitted in front of the fin to later P-51Ds – and retro-fitted to many earlier ones – to compensate and improve directional control. The P-51D also had an improved armament fit of six .5in Browning MG-53-2 machine guns; the inner guns carried 400 rounds and the center and outer ones 270 each, giving a total of 1800 rounds. All six barrels produced a total of eighty rounds a second. The prime task of the P-51s was still escorting the bombers, but the available firepower was put to good use over the Continent whenever the circumstances allowed.

The K-14 gyroscopic gun sight developed from the RAF's Gyro Gunsight Mk IID was first fitted to Colonel Donald Graham's brand new P-51D 41-3388 'Bodacious' of the 357th FG. Shortly afterward it began to replace the N-9 sight and, once mastered, provided more accurate deflection shooting. The P-51D carried the 85 US-gallon tank in its fuselage as a standard fitting. Its wings were strengthened to accept two 1000lb bombs or a combination of 500lb ones and drop tanks, or 5in High Velocity Aircraft Rockets, for which projector mountings were fitted to the last 1100 P-51Ds manufactured at Inglewood. Triple bazooka-type rocket launchers had previously been fitted.

Ferocious
Frankie

Top left: **Arming a P-51 with .5 caliber ammunition.**
Top: **Generals Auton, Eisenhower, Spaatz, Doolittle and Major General Kepner.**
Above: **A fine air-to-air shot of a P-51D over England.**

In May 1944 the first P-51Ds began to arrive in Great Britain to replace the P-51Bs and Cs in 42 USAAF Squadrons. Some pilots considered the D inferior in performance, which, with 450lb increased weight, it theoretically was. However the difference was marginal and the improved vision and fire-power more than compensated. Even so, some pilots got their ground crews to fit single or twin rear-view mirrors.

From mid-1944 American pilots began to receive the Berger G-suit. This garment automatically constricted blood supply to the lower body and limbs during high rate turns, and enabled the pilot to perform more extreme maneuvers than previously possible without blacking out. The suit was inflated by the aircraft's vacuum system. It did have the disadvantage of allowing the pilot to sustain more G than his machine could on occasions, and aircraft were known to return to base after engaging in violent combat with popped rivets and increased dihedral. Some simply disintegrated through being overstressed.

A total of 7956 P-51Ds were produced (6502 at Inglewood and 1454 at Dallas), and 281 were supplied to the RAF as Mustang IVs, while a further 594 P-51Ks also carried the same designation. One P-51D was modified in mid-1944 for deck landing trials to assess the suitability of the type for carrier operations with the United States Navy. The 44-14017 was specially strengthened and fitted with an arrester hook, and with Lieutenant R M Elder USN at the controls, successfully completed landing and takeoff trials on USS *Shangri-La* on 14 November. With 35 knots over the deck the aircraft needed only 250ft of the 855 available to become airborne. The wide-track undercarriage was advantageous, but the pilot's view from the cockpit during the approach was considered inadequate even with the seat fully raised and the project was terminated.

Four 8th Air Force Groups, each with three Squadrons, were flying the P-51 at the time of the invasion. The 4th FG was based at Debden, the 339th FG at Fowlmere, the 355th FG at Steeple Morden and the 357th FG was still at Leiston. During the night of 5 June the distinctive black and white

stripes of the Allied Expeditionary Air Force were applied to wings and fuselages, and on the following morning 355th FG machines attacked enemy transport and installations west of Paris. Little opposition was encountered from the Luftwaffe initially, and within a week of D-Day P-51Ds began to arrive.

On 2 June 1944 the first shuttle mission to Russia was flown under the command of General Eaker. One hundred and thirty B-17 bombers were escorted to the target after which they and their escorts, the 4th Fighter Group augmented by the 352nd Fighter Group's 486th Fighter Squadron and the Italian-based 15th Air Force's 325th Fighter Group all led by Donald Blakeslee, continued on to land on Russian airfields. After a seven and a half hour flight of 1470 miles during which the marshalling yards at Debreczen in Hungary were attacked, the Mustangs landed at Piryatin airfield. On 6 June the force raided Galati airfield in Rumania and returned to its Russian bases, and on 11 June the return was made to Italian bases via oil installations at Constanta and Giurgiu and the marshalling yards at Smederovo.

Above right: Major Merle J Gilbertson of 20th Fighter Group in the remains of his P-51.
Below: P-51K over the Sind Desert near Karachi.

Below: As their bombers return to base, P-51s of 353rd Fighter Group peel off to land at Raydon, Essex.

J4
J4
J4

On 21 June the second shuttle mission to Russia took place and this time escort was provided by the 8th AF's 357th Fighter Group and the 15th AF's 31st Fighter Group. The synthetic oil plant at Ruhland was attacked and the surviving 64 P-51s again landed at Piryatin after an aerial battle with about thirty German fighters near Brest-Litovsk. A simultaneous 8th raid was also launched against Berlin. On 25 June the planned return journey to Italy was cancelled because of bad weather, but the next day saw the P-51s' departure and return to Italy by way of the marshalling yards at Drohobycz. They were unable to return to the United Kingdom until 5 July, again due to bad weather conditions. Subsequent Operation Frantic missions – as these were known – took place on 7 August with attacks on Polish oil refineries and on 11 September when Chemnitz was attacked.

By July most 8th AF P-38 Lightning Squadrons had converted to the P-51, and shortly before the end of the month the first Luftwaffe jet fighters began to be encountered over Germany. Because of the Messerschmitt Me 163's high speeds, the Mustangs could not catch them except by diving, and during a raid on Magdeburg three were shot down.

On 18 August a rescue took place when First Lieutenant Royce Priest of 355th FG observed Captain Bert Marshall's P-51D force landing in a field near Soissons in France. He landed alongside the wrecked machine and picked up Marshall, on whose lap he sat for the safe return flight to England. Also in August the first Messerschmitt Me 262 jets appeared, and on 11 September the first P-51 fell to the Me's guns. On 7 October Lieutenant Urban Drew of the 376th Fighter Squadron was flying P-51D 44-14164 over Achmer airfield, home of Major Walter Nowotny's Me 262 Kommando, when he saw two taking off. He shot both down. Arado Ar 234 reconnaissance jets began to appear about the same time, and could likewise be shot down if caught unawares by P-51s flying standing patrols above their bases. A special M23 .5in incendiary round with twice the amount of incendiary composition was developed to counter the volatile German jet aircraft. Although the limited flying hours and experience of the average German fighter pilot led to many relatively 'easy' air victories, the skies above Germany were still highly dangerous and flak, particularly at low level, still took its toll.

On 18 September 355th FG Mustangs escorted B-17s to drop supplies to the beleaguered Polish partisans engaged in the Warsaw uprising. As 1944 progressed Donald Blakeslee was grounded, having flown an estimated three times the official limit of 300 combat hours. The USAAF suffered a severe loss on 25 December when Major George E Preddy, Commanding Officer of 228th Fighter Squadron, was shot down and killed by American anti-aircraft fire near Liège in Belgium in his P-51D 44-14906 'Cripes A'Mighty.' He had destroyed two Messerschmitt Me 109s earlier the same day, and shot down a total of 27 enemy aircraft, including six Me 109s in one day on 6 August. By December the 78th Fighter Group was the last 8th AF Group to convert on to the P-51. With the exception of the 56th FG (The Wolfpack) which retained its P-47s until the very end, all fourteen 8th AF Fighter Groups were flying P-51s by VE-Day.

January 1945 saw the continuation of the severe weather which had predominated the winter, and aircraft were lost because of icing, pilot fatigue and landing accidents. It also saw the arrival of the P-51K, a lightened Dallas-manufactured P-51D in which the 11ft 2in Hamilton Standard propeller was replaced by an 11ft 0in diameter lightened Aeroproducts one. Vibration problems arose and only 1500 P-51Ks were built before P-51D production was resumed. However by spring the Allies had won virtually total air superiority over Germany, and by the beginning of April the 4th Fighter Group had destroyed a total of 867 enemy aircraft on the ground and in the air. On 18 March the 359th FG encountered Russian fighters over Berlin for the first time, and during one clash a P-51D of the 353rd FG force landed after being fired at in error. Reichsmarschall Hermann Göring stated in 1945 that, when American bombers came over Berlin with fighter escort, he knew that Germany had lost the war.

Above left: **Three P-51Ds and a P-51B over England.**
Below: **P-51Bs and Ds escorting B-24 Liberators of the 8th Air Force.**

THE 2ND TAF OPERAT

The Americans by no means had a monopoly of Mustangs over Europe between 1943 and 1945. The Second Tactical Air Force of the Royal Air Force was a new command which obtained many of its pilots from the Desert Air Force. The 122nd Wing of 2 TAF was the first to equip with the Mustang, and in late December 1943 65 Squadron received the first of a total of 910 Mustang IIIs finally delivered to the RAF. These did not have the 85 US-gallon fuselage fuel tank and an immediate program of fitting Malcolm Canopies was launched. The Wing consisted of this Squadron along with 19 and 122 Squadrons, and was unfortunate to lose its Wing Leader, Wing Commander R Grant on 28 February 1944 just thirteen days after the Wing's first mission, when he suffered engine failure after takeoff and crashed on the home airdrome of Gravesend. In addition to undertaking tactical ground attack missions, the Wing also provided escorts for returning USAAF bombers but, because of the absence of the fuselage tank, could not reach far into Europe.

On 26 March two Polish Squadrons – 306 (Torunski) and 315 (Deblinski) – exchanged their Spitfire VBs for Mustangs, and 129 Squadron joined them at Coolham in Surrey in early April. These three Squadrons formed 133 Wing and, with 122 they began operations over northern France flying Ranger sorties, bomber escort missions and shipping strikes in the North Sea.

On 15 April 122 Wing moved to Ford on the south coast in readiness for the invasion, and during the build-up period and immediately afterward, both Wings devoted their attention to enemy ground targets, which exacted a heavy toll of pilots and machines. On D-Day itself the Mustangs escorted transport aircraft carrying troops across the Channel, and on 25 June aircraft of 122 Wing flew over to land at B-7 Advanced Landing Ground, and thus were the first to operate from a base on the Continent. The 133 Wing remained in the United Kingdom after the invasion, but continued to operate over occupied Europe. The Commanding Officer of 315 (Polish) Squadron, Wing Commander Eugeniusz Horbaczewski, saw one of his pilots crash land south of Cherbourg shortly after the invasion. He himself landed at a half-completed landing ground nearby, struggled across country to reach the pilot, and flew back with him to the United Kingdom. Horbaczewski was killed on 18 August, by which time he had amassed 16.5 aerial victories and shot down four V-1 flying bombs.

As the Allied armies thrust deeper into France, the Squadrons of 122 Wing followed close behind. On 15 July 19 Squadron suffered casualties to both personnel and aircraft from shelling. The RAF Mustangs again became targets for overzealous P-47 and P-38 pilots who failed to identify them. To lessen the risk, they adopted a more distinctive type of roundel incorporating white and yellow on their upper wings to augment the invasion stripes which all aircraft carried. Enemy aircraft were met and engaged and in August a series of successful attacks on barges on the Seine with 1000lb bombs was carried out to hinder German plans for the withdrawal of their ground forces; the bridges were already down.

On 28 and 29 September the three component Squadrons of 122 Wing were brought back to the United Kingdom and joined 150 Wing at Matlaske in Norfolk as part of the Air Defence of Great Britain force. From then on they were to escort RAF bombers on daylight raids under the operational control of No 11 and No 13 Groups, and their place in France was taken by 2 TAF Tempest Squadrons. While in France they had destroyed 93 German aircraft and countless ground targets had been dealt with.

As part of the reconnaissance element of 2 TAF, Mustang Is were operated by three Royal Canadian Air Force Squadrons. The 83 Group had 400 Squadron at Redhill and 414 and 430 Squadrons at Gatwick, 84 Group had four RAF Squadrons under its control, 2 and 4 Squadrons at Odiham and 168 and 268 Squadrons at Thruxton. Two out of the three Groups belonging to 2 TAF under the command of Air Marshal Arthur Coningham were equipped with Mustangs.

In November 1943 the RAF Squadrons, with the exception of 268, combined to form 35 (Reconnaissance) Wing based at Sawbridgeworth. Every opportunity was taken by the RAF and RCAF pilots to engage the enemy as well as to photograph him, and in readiness for the invasion a program of systematic reconnaissance began in early 1944. Three Mustang Squadrons trained for Naval Shore Bombardment Spotting carried out this task on D-Day, although two Mustangs fell to Spitfires whose pilots had failed to recognize them.

In June the Mark I Mustangs began to be replaced by Mark IIs and commenced a series of tactical reconnaissance (Tac R) missions which were again interrupted by friendly fighters, but managed to acquire much valuable information. The Mustang was also used by Group Captain Leonard Cheshire VC, DSO and 2 bars, DFC as a target marking aircraft for the pinpoint bombing attacks of 617 Squadron which he commanded. Taking full advantage of the Mustang's maneuverability and range he flew one modified to carry smoke markers to a V-2 rocket site at Siracourt in France in June 1944 and successfully marked it from low level. In July he flew two similar sorties, to Creil and Mimoyecques for marking an ammunition dump and an underground long-range artillery position respectively. Unable to obtain a Mustang from his own Service, Cheshire borrowed one from the USAAF, and when he was posted his successor carried on the tradition.

On 18 June 1944 the Germans launched 22 V-1 (Vergeltungswaffe, or Reprisal weapon) flying bombs at London, and countermeasures were immediately taken. The 122 Wing flew to France later in the month, but 133 Wing was available and was able to use its Mustang IIIs in Operation Diver against the new threat. To augment the Gun Belt stretching from Beachy Head to Dover which was hurriedly deployed by General Sir Frederick Pile, GOC of Anti-Aircraft Command, Mustangs flew standing patrols off Kent over the Channel, and the pilots were vectored on to their targets by a radar controller. At night searchlights were used for target illumination. The V-1s mostly flew at heights between 2–3000ft, and fighters were ordered to fly no lower than 8000ft to allow a margin of safety from the guns which engaged targets crossing the coast at lower altitude. V-1s were small targets and flew at 380mph. Trial and error determined the best technique for dealing with them, which was to approach

ONS

from astern and open fire from 350 yards, whereupon with luck the target would explode and the attacker could fly through the debris unscathed.

A successful exponent of this dangerous art was Warrant Officer Tadeusz Szymanski of 316 (Warszawski) Polish Squadron who destroyed nine V-1s including some whose gyros he caused to topple by formating alongside the flying bomb and gently raising his Mustang's wing tip against the underside of the target's. His Squadron, flown down from Coltishall in Norfolk to augment the defenses along with Meteors, Spitfires and Tempests, destroyed 74 V-1s. Attempts were made to boost the power of the Merlin by using 130-octane fuel, but this caused valves to burn out, and the only way that Mustangs could reliably attack the bombs was by diving to achieve the necessary speed. As the majority of the launching sites were overrun by September 1944, the danger temporarily passed, but V-1s soon began to arrive from the east, and the Diver Belt Gun Box defenses were increased to extend from the Thames Estuary to Great Yarmouth in Norfolk. In all 232 flying bombs were destroyed by Mustangs.

In October 1944 122 and 133 Wings combined to form a seven-squadron unit based at Andrews Field, also known as Great Saling, near Chelmsford in Essex. The seventh squadron was 316 from Coltishall. From Andrews Field they provided escorts for RAF day bombing attacks and in December they were joined by a further expanded Wing of six RAF Squadrons converted to Mustang IIIs and based at Bentwaters in Suffolk. This brought the total of RAF Mustangs to nearly 250. The first Messerschmitt Me 262 fell to an RAF Mustang in late March 1945.

In February 1945 the RAF finally obtained the P-51D and called it the Mustang Mark IV; the Americans had received it in the United Kingdom as early as May the previous year. It equipped the third planned Mustang Wing at Hunsdon in Hertfordshire, which never reached full strength by the time hostilities ended. Most Mustang IVs flew in bare metal finish, and carried the red, white and blue upper wing roundels introduced on 3 January 1945. The first RAF Squadron to receive the Mustang IV was 303 (Kosciuszko) Polish Squadron, and the RAF eventually received 281 P-51Ds and the later K version both of which carried the Mark IV designation.

This Mustang re-equipped two Mustang III Squadrons which had flown their earlier Marks as escorts to Mosquito and Beaufighter shipping strikes off the Norwegian coast. These operations were flown at sea level, and involved a round trip of some 1000 miles from the airdrome at Peterhead near Aberdeen. Two RAF Mustang Squadrons were involved, 19 and 65 Squadrons from 122 Wing. Over Norway they met spirited opposition from the Luftwaffe, many of whose experienced pilots were sent there for rest and recuperation. These operations subjected the Mustang pilots to great strain, since even momentary failure of the Merlin would mean the aircraft hitting the sea, and the quality of the opposition awaiting them was more predictable than over the skies of Germany where, by this stage in the war, many German fighter pilots had very little flying experience. In August 1944 the USAAF's 4th Fighter Group participated in several sorties, but the bulk of this flying was done by the RAF until the end of the war. On 16 April 1945 Mustang IVs of 611 Squadron encountered Russian fighters over Berlin. When the German High Command surrendered unconditionally on 7 May 1945, the sixteen RAF Mustang Squadrons had some 320 aircraft available and the USAAF about 1600 in Europe.

Below: **Group Captain Leonard Cheshire, VC, DSO, DFC used P-51s to pinpoint targets on bombing raids.**

Below: **Relaxing at an advanced landing ground following the Normandy invasion.**

ITALIAN OPERATIONS

In November 1943 the United States 15th Air Force was designated the Mediterranean theater strategic bomber force, and relied initially upon three P-38 Lightning Groups and subsequently one P-47 Thunderbolt Group as fighter escort in the 306th Fighter Wing. The 15th Air Force had been created on 1 November 1943 under the command of Major General James H Doolittle. The 12th Air Force with which it operated was a tactical formation which had been instituted in August 1942, as the American counterpart to the RAF's Desert Air Force, to provide support for the US 5th Army. In December 1943 it was incorporated into the newly-formed Mediterranean Allied Air Forces. With the expansion of the bomber force new escort groups were soon needed, and on 2 April 1944 the 31st Fighter Group received its first P-51Bs as replacements for the Spitfires previously used. Two weeks later they flew to Rumania on their first escort operation, and on 21 April the 31st FG escorted a raid on the Ploesti oil refineries north of Bucharest, during the course of which they shot down seventeen enemy aircraft. The 31st was commanded by Major James Thorsen. In May the second 15th AF Mustang Group, the 52nd, received its machines, and the 325th exchanged its P-47s shortly afterward to form the third. It was the last-mentioned Fighter Group – the Checkertails – which helped escort the first shuttle mission to Russian bases on 2 June 1944. On the day the Allied invasion was launched along the French Channel coast, the 325th escorted their bombers on the raid on Galati in Rumania.

The 52nd Fighter Group succeeded in shooting down thirteen German fighters without loss during a raid on Munich three days later, and the 31st Fighter Group took part in the second shuttle mission, along with P-38s, on 21 June 1944. During their short stay in Russia and before the return journey to San Severo was made, they took part in an aerial battle over Poland in which the Mustangs engaged a force of 41 German aircraft, mainly Junkers Ju87s, and shot down 27 confirmed.

In June 1944 the 332nd Fighter Group received its first Mustangs. This unit was an all-Negro one and its red-tailed and spinnered P-51s were based at Foggia. During July, August and September much ground strafing was carried out, and on 31 August the 52nd FG was sent to attack the Luftwaffe airfield at Reghin in Rumania, and destroyed over 150 enemy machines as the Mustangs flew pass after pass over the devastated area. In three days (30 August–1 September) 193 P-51s claimed a total of 211 enemy aircraft destroyed and a further 131 damaged on four Rumanian airfields. The 325th FG attacked another airfield at Ecka in Yugoslavia on 10 September and destroyed forty aircraft. During a strafing attack by the 31st FG a rescue similar to the ones carried out by Royce Priest and Eugeniusz Horbaczewski took place when Lieutenant Charles E Wilson force-landed his P-51 after it was damaged when a train he was attacking exploded. Major Wyatt P Exum landed nearby and picked him up.

During the autumn and winter of 1944 opposition in the air over the Balkans declined, although the P-51 Groups continued to harry ground targets, but on 14 March 1945 the 325th was involved in a great air battle over Hungary with 35 Focke Wulf Fw 190s. Two P-51s were lost for the destruction of seventeen of the enemy. Ten days later all four Mustang Groups combined to escort a bomber force to Berlin and back – a round trip of over 1500 miles. On the return journey Colonel William Daniel, Commanding Officer of 308th FS of the 31st FG, engaged a Messerschmitt Me 262 and shot it down, while six others were shot down on the same day, three by the 332nd FG. This Group also claimed thirteen enemy aircraft destroyed in a fight near Linz in Austria.

In March 1944 260 Squadron RAF exchanged its P-40 Kittyhawks for Mustang IIIs. This Desert Air Force Squadron was based at Cutella in the south of Italy and collected its machines

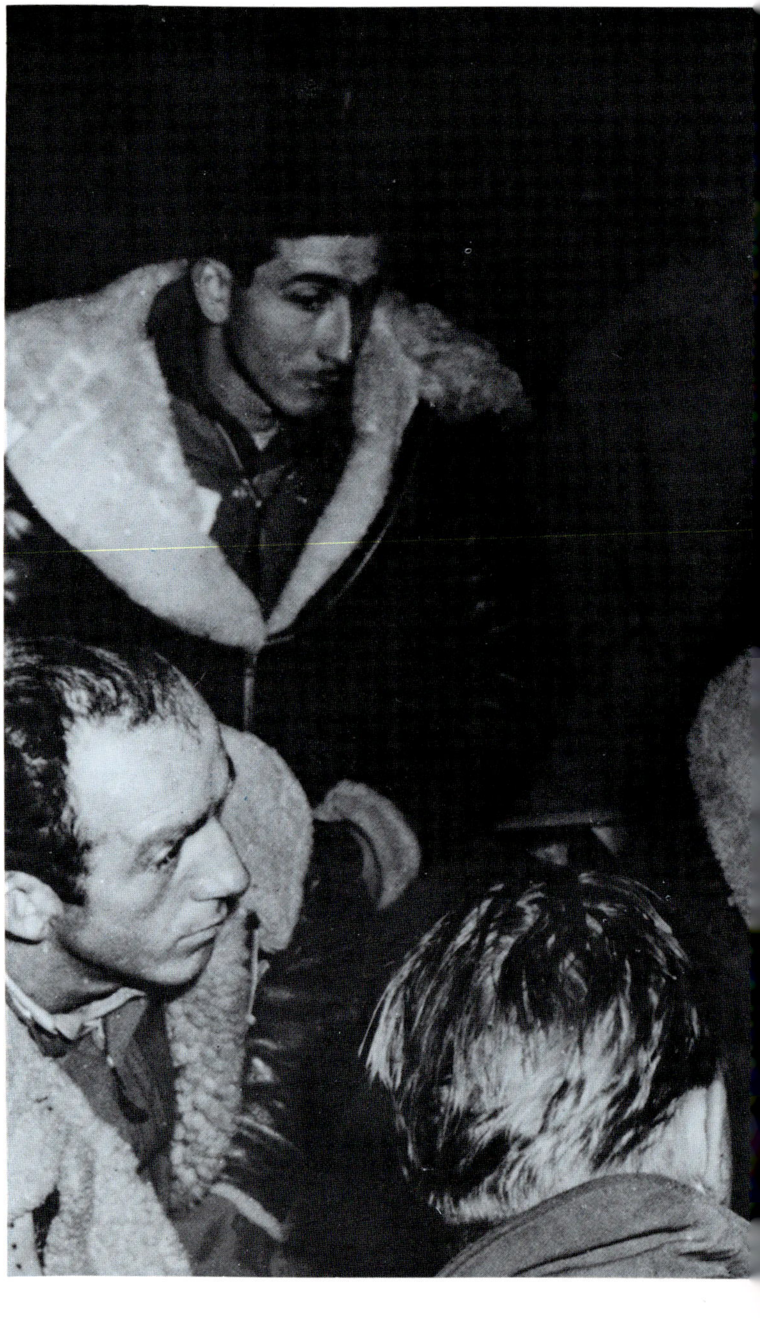

from Casablanca. In May the Squadron attacked and breached the Pescara dam, and the resulting floods enabled the British 8th Army to provide support for the US 5th Army, because the former's right flank was protected by the water. July saw the equipping of 112 and 213 Squadrons with Mustangs, and ground attack missions were flown for both armies. The 112 Squadron had flown Kittyhawks and continued to display on its Mustangs the sharks' teeth insignia carried on its predecessors'. In September 249 Squadron and 5 Squadron South African Air Force received Mustangs and 3 Squadron RAAF equipped with them in November. The 112, 213 and 249 Squadrons were all re-equipped with Mustang IVs.

All six squadrons operated over the Balkans, primarily engaged in ground support tasks. To this end they carried two 1000lb bombs, thereby doubling the recommended bomb load, but the wings of the Mustang were strong enough to carry the extra weight. Rocket projectiles were also fitted and used to good effect. However, as the Americans had found, there was little opposition in the sky, and after the last winter of the war it was apparent that the enemy in Europe was defeated.

Below: **Lieutenant General Carl Spaatz (right) debriefs an Italian-based American bomber crew just returned from a mission over Austria.**

CHINA-BURMA-INDIA

The Mustang's first appearance in India was with the 311th Fighter Group of the United States 10th Air Force in October 1943. This consisted of 528, 529 and 530th Fighter Squadrons. The Group had 40 A-36A dive bombers divided between two squadrons, and the third was equipped with P-51A Allison Mustangs. It operated from Dinjan and flew missions against the Japanese in northern Burma from northeast India, and protected the air route to China, where P-51Bs were to equip the United States 14th Air Force, which was commanded by Major General Claire L Chennault. He had raised the American Volunteer Group in November 1940 in the United States which flew under the operational control of the Chinese Air Force from December 1941 until 4 July 1942, when it was finally incorporated into the 23rd Fighter Group. In this period, flying Curtiss P-40B and E Warhawks, the AVG destroyed 286 Japanese aircraft. This included 6.5 shot down by the then Captain James Howard. The air route took Allied transport 'over the Hump' with essential supplies and the P-51's range was put to good use.

The P-51As of 530th FS deployed south to Kurmitola in Bengal, from where they escorted B-25 Mitchell and B-24 Liberator bombers in attacks on Rangoon. To provide sufficient range two 75 US-gallon drop tanks were carried. Losses were high however; in November Colonel Harry Melton, the commander of the 311th FG, was lost, and the heavily laden P-51As were found to be at a disadvantage when confronted by Japanese Nakajima Ki-43 Oscar and Nakajima Ki-44 Tojo fighters. The attack during which he was lost was aimed at the home airfield of the Japanese 64th Sentai, which provided fighter defense for the area. During the winter of 1943 enemy lines of communication continued to be attacked, and escort was provided for aerial supply missions to Chinese forces moving southward down the Hukawng Valley. In early March 1944 the Group also began operations in support of Merrill's Marauders in the same area. During these operations the ground forces made use of Army Air Force Forward Air Controllers to call down air strikes just ahead of the troops, with notable accuracy and success. The Japanese retaliated by trying to destroy the 311th FG's base but their air attacks were repulsed.

The P-51As also equipped two Air Commando Units which were employed to provide air support for Major General Orde Wingate's Chindits who operated behind Japanese lines. Their tasks included carrying a 1000lb bomb or triple rocket launchers mounted beneath each wing for ground attack, and a cable was sometimes trailed to destroy Japanese telephone and power lines. These Mustangs operated under difficult conditions from rough strips and performed most useful work.

In April 1944 the first Merlin-engined P-51Bs began to arrive to equip the 311th FG at Dinjan, but the bulk of Mustang production was directed toward Europe. In May 1944 one squadron of the Group was sent to Dohazari to disrupt attempts made by the Japanese to resupply their troops at

Right: **P-51s with distinctive recognition markings over the Chin Hills in Burma, on a mission to destroy Japanese supply depots.**

THEATER OPERATIONS

Above: **A P-51 of the Flying Tigers with triple rocket launchers.**
Above right: **Col Tex Hill, CO of 23rd Fighter Group and his P-51 at Kweilin, China.**
Right: **Curtiss P-40 Warhawk as used by the AVG. The P-51 superseded the P-40.**

Myitkina and Imphal. In four days it shot down 24 Japanese aircraft without losing a single Mustang, a sign of the increasing American air superiority.

In China the 23rd Fighter Group had been re-equipped with Merlin-engined Mustangs by December 1944 and the 311th FG moved these from India to begin operating from an advanced landing ground at Hsian in Northern China. Here as everywhere else conditions were spartan and all supplies had to come by air. Much improvisation and the use of coolie labor enabled the fighters to keep flying. Modifications included the fitting of two 250lb bomb racks outboard of the 75 US-gallon drop tanks, provision for eighteen antipersonnel bombs on racks outboard of three 100lb bomb mountings beneath each wing and a total of four 75 US-gallon drop tanks which, including the capacity of the 85 US-gallon fuselage tank, provided a range of 2700 miles. With this extreme range Japanese targets could be attacked which had previously been immune. The 311th FG – known as the Yellow Scorpions – rotated its squadrons through Hsian, and on 24 December 1944 the 530th FS carried out a spectacular attack on Tsinan airfield, destroying some eighty Japanese aircraft on this and two subsequent raids.

The 23rd Fighter Group based at Kweilin also carried out constant strafing and bombing attacks both on shipping and land targets, as well as escorting medium-range American bombers. The Group was joined by the 118th Tactical Reconnaissance Squadron in mid-1944, which soon began to develop a skip-bombing technique not normally included in the repertoire of a reconnaissance unit. On 8 December thirteen Mustangs successfully raided Hong Kong harbor using 500lb bombs, and on the return journey shot up the Japanese airfield at Tok Pak Uk.

Major John C Herbst – known as Pappy because of his relatively advanced years – commanded the 74th FS of the 23rd FG. He flew a P-51B (43-7060) 'Tommy's Dad,' and between July 1944 and February 1945 he shot down twenty Japanese aircraft to add to his single German victory from North Africa, and thus became the highest scoring American pilot in the theater. Another successful exponent of the P-51 was Colonel Ed McComas, who shot down fourteen.

The Royal Air Force intended to use Mustang IVs in Burma, but the war ended before the several hundred which were shipped to India and assembled at Dum Dum airfield near Calcutta could be brought into action. The Mustang – of which there were never more than 500 in the CBI theater – had again proved its versatility in far from ideal conditions and, as in Europe, had used its great range for escorting bombers and transports as well as reaching far behind enemy lines. And it still had one more important part to play in the Southwest Pacific.

TURBO-THREE
26
26

THE PACIFIC

Not until late 1944 did General George C Kenney, Commander of the United States 5th Air Force in the Southwest Pacific area, receive any Mustangs. The first were F-6D reconnaissance aircraft which were assigned to the 82nd Tac R Squadron of the 71st Reconnaissance Group, stationed at San Jose Field at Mindoro in the Philippines. On 11 January 1945 Captain William A Shomo was leading a pair of F-6Ds with First Lieutenant Paul N Lipscomb as his wingman on a reconnaissance mission to Japanese airfields in North Luzon. As they drew near to their target area they spotted a formation of enemy aircraft consisting of a single Mitsubishi G4M Betty bomber containing, presumably, some eminent Japanese since it was escorted by no less than twelve Kawasaki Ki-61 Tony fighters. Despite the enemy's numerical superiority, the two American pilots turned to attack, and in the ensuing melee Captain Shomo shot down the bomber and six fighters, while his wingman dispatched a further four. For his bravery and success Shomo was awarded the Congressional Medal of Honor.

In January 1945 the Third Air Commando Group received its first P-51Ds. By this time there was not much Japanese air activity over the Philippines, and the squadrons of the Group were able to pursue their primary task of low-level ground attack on Japanese tactical targets and communications.

On 19 February 1945 United States Marines invaded the island of Iwo Jima, and a 36-day battle of unparallelled ferocity began. The Japanese had about 23,000 soldiers on the island, well dug in, and with a complex of tunnels from which they would emerge to attack the American rear. When the battle was over American dead numbered 6821 and only 1083 Japanese were taken prisoner. No sooner had a foothold been gained than Seabees (Construction Battalions) moved in to establish a landing ground for the P-51Ds of the 15th and 21st FGs. These units were to escort the B-29 Superfortress bombers of the United States Twentieth Bomber Command on their raids against the Japanese homeland. The B-29s had already launched raids on Japan from their bases at Saipan and Tinian in the Marianas, but without fighter escort.

On 6 March the 15th FG arrived on the South Field of Iwo Jima, and on 15 March the 21st FG joined them. At a cost of the most appalling USMC casualty figures, a base was now available from which the P-51s could escort the bombers along the 700 or so miles to Japan; but before the first escort mission was flown, the Mustangs provided air support for the Marines both on the island and on others nearby. The Japanese were still offering resistance, and on occasions the North Field airstrip came under attack and American Squadron personnel were killed. The fields themselves consisted of volcanic rock whose dust, in addition to causing visibility problems after the slipstream of aircraft taxying and taking off had created swirling clouds of it, also acted as a fine abrasive and clogged filters. As ever, the ground crews soldiered on in thoroughly unpleasant, sometimes dangerous but unspectacular conditions, to ensure that their machines were on top line, as they did in all other theaters.

On 7 April the first escort mission to Japan was flown when 96 P-51Ds from the six component squadrons of both Fighter Groups took off and set course to rendezvous with a force of over 100 B-29s. The Mustangs carried two 110 US-gallon metal drop tanks pressurized by the aircraft's vacuum pump, but even so they had little time to loiter over their target, the Nakajima aircraft factory in the capital city, Tokyo. To ease navigation problems an escort B-29 was provided on both legs, and only one P-51 was lost on this first raid. Due to the vast distances involved and the unpredictability of the weather, special weather flights preceded the main force, and

Above: Fifth Air Force 35th Fighter Group aircraft taxi out in the Philippines.
Left: 45th Fighter Squadron, 15th Fighter Group armorers replenish a P-51's guns.
Below: P-51D prepares to take off from Iwo Jima.
Bottom: 'Bore-sighting' a 41st Fighter Squadron P-51s guns at Clark Field, Luzon in 1945.

the B-29 shepherd aircraft carried life rafts in case an American pilot was forced to come down in the sea. If he did so, his chances of survival were good, since the United States Navy had pre-positioned submarines to pick him up along the route. All of this must have been very reassuring to the pilot of a single-engined fighter when faced with flights of many hours duration over the Pacific Ocean. Both Groups encountered strong enemy resistance on the first raid, but shot down 21 Japanese aircraft for the loss of only three B-29s.

On 16 April the first strafing attack was launched on the Japanese home island of Kyushu. This was another flight of nearly 800 miles each way and was successful. In another raid four days later Major James B Tapp of the 15th FG shot down his fifth enemy aircraft over Japan and achieved 'ace' status when his and the 21st FG were sent to attack airfields at Yokosuka and Atgui. In May the 506th Fighter Group added its P-51Ds to those of the other two Groups and on one of its first missions with them on 1 June 1945 was unfortunate to encounter a vast frontal system reaching from sea level to well over 20,000ft. A total of 148 Mustangs took off to escort a B-29 force to Osaka, but two hours later they flew into the towering clouds associated with this front. In the ensuing turbulence and zero visibility collisions occurred, aircraft broke up, pilots became completely disoriented as their instruments toppled and airframes iced up. The squadrons were hopelessly split up; under thirty picked up their formation and continued toward their rendezvous with the bombers off Japan, over ninety aborted and returned to Iwo Jima and some 25 were lost. This was the greatest air disaster to befall the Americans in this theater. The Groups consolidated and continued to harass Japanese industry and airfields. Opposition became increasingly stubborn and large numbers of fighters met the attackers in the closing months of the war. At 0815 hours local time on 6 August 1945 the first atomic bomb exploded over Hiroshima, and on 9 August the second was dropped over Nagasaki. The war was over.

The Mustang had flown distances which no one just under five years earlier would have believed possible for a single-engined fighter, or its pilots; sometimes over eight hours elapsed before a weary fighter pilot in his early twenties would bring his aircraft over the fence at 110mph and feel the reassuring rumble of ground beneath his wheels. In the intervening war years the Mustang had destroyed 4950 enemy aircraft in the air and a further 4131 on the ground.

Right: **Republic P-47 Thunderbolt, Lockheed P-38 Lightning and P-51D Mustang.**
Below right: **Major Robert W Moore, CO of a P-51 squadron on Iwo Jima.**
Below: **P-51D and B-29 Superfortress rendezvous off the Japanese coast, July 1945.**

Stinger VII

PROTOTYPES AND PO

The development of the P-51 from the Allison-engined A version via the B, C and D had been accompanied by a steady increase in weight; the P-51A weighed 6433lb empty and the P-51D 7125lb. By way of comparison, a Spitfire V weighed only 5050lb. With a view to producing a lighter machine, Edgar Schmued led a group of engineers from North American to Great Britain in early 1943 to study British design techniques. As a result of their findings, North American proposed a lighter version and a contract for three prototypes was approved in July. These were designated XP-51F, G and J. The first incorporated a new laminar flow wing and components were redesigned and lightened. A new and lighter undercarriage was housed in a wing which had a straighter leading edge, the canopy was extended and the oil cooler was replaced by a heat exchanger. A three-bladed Aeroproducts propeller with hollow blades was fitted to the standard 1450hp Packard Merlin V-1650 7 engine of the P-51D. The fuselage fuel tank was omitted and the armament reduced to four .5in Brownings. A weight saving of 1300lb had been intended, and when the first P-51F took to the air on 14 February 1944 it weighed 5635lb empty, which represented a weight reduction of 1490lb. Not surprisingly its performance was considerably enhanced, and the P-51F added 30mph to its predecessor's maximum speed of 437mph. The RAF had requested one for evaluation and received one of the three produced in June, which became FR 409. Had it been accepted it would have become the Mustang V, but the machine was not without vices and no further examples were built.

The P-51G carried a Rolls-Royce Merlin 100 engine with a five-bladed British Rotol propeller. Two were produced and one (FR 410) was supplied to the RAF who obtained a maximum speed of just under 500mph from it at 20,000ft, a height to which it could climb in a breathtaking 3.4 minutes.

The P-51J reverted to the Allison V-1710-119 engine and performed well, but again only two were built. It was from experience with the P-51F that the lightweight production model, the P-51H, was developed. The H version was powered by a 1380hp Packard Merlin V-1650-9 with water injection and driving a four-bladed constant speed Aeroproducts propeller, which gave it a speed of 487mph at 25,000ft. To improve directional stability the fin was enlarged and the dorsal strake which had been omitted on the F was replaced. The D-type canopy was fitted and the two 105 US-gallon wing tanks were augmented by a 50 US-gallon fuselage one. The weight saving on the P-51D was in the region of 1000lb and the armament fit was either four or six .50in Brownings. Only 555 P-51Hs were built before the end of the war brought construction to a halt, and only a few had reached the Pacific theater by then.

A planned P-51L would have carried an uprated Packard Merlin V-1650-11 but the project was cancelled and the last P-51 produced was the M, an H without water injection, of which a single example was built at Dallas in September 1945.

Perhaps the most interesting project which arose during the war was for a long-range escort fighter consisting of two P-51H fuselages joined together. This design was prompted by

STWAR

Above: Air-to-air view of the lightweight production P-51H.
Above right: One of three P-51Fs supplied to the RAF.
Below: Prototype lightweight XP-51F showing the enlarged canopy.

the desire to reduce pilot fatigue during prolonged flights in the Pacific Theater, and the prospect of doubling the crew of an already proven aircraft obviated the time-consuming and costly development program of a completely new type. When North American suggested the idea as the XP-82, the USAAF accepted and four prototypes were ordered on 7 January 1944. The first flight took place in Los Angeles on 15 April 1945.

In the XP-82 Twin Mustang two P-51H fuselages were joined by a common center-wing section and inboard horizontal stabilizer; the outer stabilizers were deleted. The pilot of the combination sat in the port fuselage and the second pilot in the starboard. The former had a full range of instruments and the latter sufficient to take over should the need arise, or to act as navigator. The armament of six .5in Brownings was housed in the center section of the wing, and the outer wings carried pylons for one 1000lb bomb or 310 US-gallon drop tanks. Interval tanks housed 576 US-gallons which, with drop tanks, gave a maximum range of some 4000 miles.

The P-82B of early 1945 was the first production model and was powered by two 1380hp Packard Merlin V-1650-9 engines with propellers rotating in an inward direction. Some were converted into P-82C and D night fighter versions as a replacement for the Northrop P-61 Black Widow, and the P-82E was a long-range escort fighter with Allison V-1710 engines and autopilot. The F was a photographic reconnaissance and night fighter variant carrying a pod for the AN/APG-28 radar beneath its center section. This arrived in squadron service in 1948; in July 1947 the US Army Air Force had changed its name to the United States Air Force and in June 1948 the USAF changed the designation P (Pursuit) to F (Fighter). So the P-82F became the F-82F and both this and the F-51 saw action in Korea.

The TP-51D was a two-seater trainer version of the P-51D and ten were built. Several war weary P-51Bs with WW on their tails, had been converted unofficially into two-seaters, some with additional Malcolm hoods, but the large blister canopy of the D provided sufficient room for a second seat if the radio was moved into the rear fuselage. The TP-51Ds maximum all-up weight was 11,300lb.

With the cessation of hostilities in 1945 production was run down; in September the North American plant at Dallas ceased P-51 production and in November Inglewood followed suit. The United Kingdom-based squadrons departed and in East Anglia many former Mustang bases reverted to farmland. In America P-51s were available on the war-surplus market at one-fifteenth of their original production cost, but other

Above: **Twin Mustang in flight.**
Below: **Twin Mustang–the F-82 showing its substantial armament.**

Above: **TP-51 – the two-seater trainer version of which ten were produced. It was used to train pilots for service in the Pacific.**

Above: **Australian license-built CA-17 Mustang 20 series aircraft equipped the RAAF after 1945.**

models remained in first-line USAF service to until the 1950s. The Air National Guard fighter squadrons were equipped with Ds and Hs for a decade postwar, while Mustang IVs flew with the RAF until May 1947.

While American production ceased, Australia was still producing P-51Ds under license as CA-17 Mustang 20s at the Commonwealth Aircraft Corporation near Melbourne. Tooling-up had begun in February 1945, and on 29 April the first CA-17 was airborne. Two hundred were eventually built, some with 1450hp Merlin 68 engines known as Mustang 21s, while the 22 was a PR version, and the 23 carried British-built Merlin engines. A further 298 were provided by the United States under Lend-Lease agreements. Mustangs were flown by three regular RAAF squadrons in early 1946.

As part of the occupation forces in Japan the 81st Wing consisted of 76, 77 and 82 Squadrons, and the Mustang equipped the five reserve squadrons of the Citizen Air Force in Australia until the late 1950s. Canada also continued to fly the Mustang for a few years after the war had ended, ordering 130 between 1947 and 1951 for use with the Royal Canadian Auxiliary Air Force; the Royal New Zealand Air Force acquired thirty in 1951 to equip the Territorial Air Force.

Mustangs continued to serve in many air forces after the war. The United States had supplied 50 P-51Ds to the Chinese

Above: **F-51D of the Italian Air Force resting on perforated steel plate sheets.**

Nationalist Air Force before Japan surrendered, and they obtained many more from surplus USAF stocks before withdrawing to Formosa. The Chinese Communists captured some which were left behind on the mainland, but the Nationalists had two F-51D and one RF-51D Squadrons in December 1954.

The Royal Swedish Air Force evaluated two P-51Bs and two P-51Ds (including one belonging to the US 8th AFs 339th FG) which had infringed Sweden's neutral air space during the war, and had been interned. Impressed by the aircraft, they ordered 157 P-51Ds as the J26, which were supplied between April 1945 and March 1948. From surplus Swedish stocks the Dominican Air Force obtained 42 in 1952, which flew as fighter bombers until 1978. Such longevity says a great deal for the strength of the design.

Israel received 25 between November 1952 and the spring of 1953 from the same source, and flew them until 1960; during the battles of 1956 they flew ground attack missions against the Egyptians. The Nicaraguan Air Force also bought 26 ex-Swedish P-51Ds in November 1954 and operated them for eleven years.

Under the terms of the Rio Pact, the United States supplied Mustangs to several countries in the Caribbean and South America in the immediate postwar years. Cuba operated some until 1960 and the Guatemalan and Haitian Air Forces received a few. The latter retains six to this day, while the former operated theirs until 1972. Uruguay acquired 25 P-51Ds in 1950 and flew them for ten years. The Air Forces of El Salvador, Honduras and Bolivia also flew small numbers.

The Armée de l'Air of France received P-51Ds for its 33rd Reconnaissance Wing in February 1945. Switzerland purchased some 140 in 1948 and operated them for ten years, and

Below: **This P-51D Mustang (N991R) was modified for air racing which has developed since the war as a popular pastime.**

Below: **P-51D photographed at an air display in England. P-51Ds were bought up cheaply after World War II.**

Above: **P-51D (N10601) photographed at Dulles Airport, Washington DC.**

Italy obtained 48 in the same year and flew them for a similar period, finally selling some to Somalia. The Royal Netherlands Air Force flew Mustangs postwar in the Dutch East Indies where forty were flown by 121 and 122 Squadrons against Indonesian forces in 1948–49. With the advent of peace the Dutch handed over their remaining stocks to their former enemies, who still operate some. The Philippine and South Korean Air Forces also acquired small numbers.

In the same era the American National Air Races were revived and large numbers of surplus P-51s were enthusiastically adopted by air racing pilots who recognized the aircraft's potential at once. The Bendix Trophy Race of 1946 was won by Paul Mantz in NX 1202, a P-51C conversion which covered the 2048 miles from Van Nuys in California to Cleveland Municipal Airport at an average speed of 435.5mph, and second and third places were also taken by P-51Cs. Throughout the late 1940s Mustangs battled with P-38 Lightnings and F-6 Corsairs, ever improving their power output. The 1949 Bendix Trophy was won by Joe De Bona's F-6C conversion at a speed of 470.1mph; like Paul Mantz he had fitted a 'wet wing,' in which all available internal space had been converted into a fuel reservoir. The Korean War effectively brought air racing to a stop in 1950, and not until the early 1960s did it enjoy a revival when P-51s again proved their worth in races held at Reno, Nevada in 1964. The following year saw Reno established as the home of American air racing when the National Championship Air Races were held there. The contestants were now mainly P-51Ds, again heavily modified. In 1975 one P-51D appeared powered by a 2445hp Rolls-Royce Griffon 57 engine with a de Havilland six-bladed contra-rotating propeller. In the United Kingdom Charles Masefield flew a P-51D to win the 1967 King's Cup Air Race, and won several other races in the same year.

Below: **A P-51D in the markings of the 83rd Fighter Squadron of the 78th Fighter Group, 8th Air Force.**

Below: **P-51D (N6306T) postwar at Reading, Pennsylvania. Air racing was revived again after the Korean War.**

KOREA AND AFTER

On 25 June 1950 the North Koreans crossed the 38th parallel and invaded South Korea, thus beginning the Korean War. The nearest United Nations air forces were based in Japan, where the Royal Australian Air Force's 77 Squadron was still stationed at Iwakuni – although its two sister squadrons had been withdrawn to Australia only the previous year. On 2 July they flew their first operational mission escorting USAF B-29 bombers over the North. The 77 Squadron was sent to South Korea and ultimately moved into the North. Until April 1951 saw the re-equipping of the Squadron with Meteor F.8s it flew many ground attack missions over inhospitable mountainous terrain which offered little chance of a successful forced landing, and the old vulnerability of the liquid-cooled engine to ground fire was rediscovered.

The South African Air Force also flew P-51Ds in the Korean War although it had not operated the type previously. Having converted at Johnson Air Force Base near Tokyo, its single squadron – 2 (Cheetah) Squadron – flew its first operation on 19 November 1950 attached to the USAF's 18th Fighter Bomber Group, and continued to fly P-51s until January 1953. It also engaged in low-level operations and lost nearly sixty Mustangs to enemy ground fire. In addition to the hostile environment, the piston-engined fighters had to contend with Russian-built MiG-15 jets and the United States rated the all-volunteer South African Squadron's efforts so highly that it was awarded a Presidential Unit Citation for 'extraordinary heroism.'

The United States Air Force had, of course, retained F-51s postwar, and both these and the F-82 Twin Mustang were available when the Korean War broke out. The 347th (All-Weather) Fighter Group was based at Itazuke in Japan and in June 1950 consisted of the 4th, 68th and 339th Fighter Squadrons. On 27 June an F-82G piloted by Lieutenant William G Hudson of 68th FS scored the first American aerial victory of the war by shooting down a North Korean Yak-9 fighter during a mission providing top cover for the evacuation of Americans near Seoul in South Korea. Four others were dispatched in the same fight.

The F-51D was flown by the 8th, 35th and 49th Fighter Bomber Groups during the early days of the war and the 18th FB Group operated it until January 1953. The 45th Tactical Reconnaissance Squadron flew RF-51s from September 1950 until the Armistice in July 1953. Altogether the Americans employed some 250 F-51Ds in the ground-attack role and, as did all the UN Mustang Squadrons, suffered very heavy losses. But the Mustang was the only aircraft available in quantity which had the necessary range and endurance and could carry sufficient weapons to inflict damage. Various combinations of bombs and 5in HVAR RPs in multiples of three were carried, along with the effective battery of six .5in Brownings. There was still a use for the piston-engined fighter in the jet age, and the American F-80 Shooting Stars were not as well suited to low-level operations. Major Louis J Sebille, Commanding Officer of the 67th FS, won a posthumous Congressional Medal of Honor in an F-51D on 5 August 1950 when, mortally wounded, he continued to press home an attack on ground forces near Pusan and finally crashed his aircraft straight into his objective.

Above: An F-51D releases its napalm over a North Korean target in August 1951.
Top: As his family watches, Captain Johnnie Gosnell taxies his F-82 in Japan.

Above: Ilyushin Il-2 falls to the guns of an F-51 flown by Lt-Col Ralph D Saltman.
Below: South African Cheetah Squadron aircraft returns from a mission.

Right: **The arrival at Wright-Patterson AFB of the last ANG F-51 on 27 January 1957, where one example is displayed. Major James L Miller is the pilot.**
Far right: **A USAF F-51 still airborne in 1978 – one of very few used as chase planes.**

The Korean War really saw the demise of the F-51 as a combat aircraft, however, and the one attempt to convert it into a counterinsurgency machine did not lead to its adoption. The Trans-Florida Aviation Company of Sarasota undertook a program of F-51D conversion in 1961. The D was given a second seat and called the Cavalier 2000. It was aimed at providing an executive aircraft capable of high-speed cruising over long ranges, with an element of excitement lacking in more pedestrian civil aircraft designs. For instance, the executive could subject his client to up to +9G at speeds not exceeding 490mph, and he could cruise at 424mph at 30,000ft. The Cavalier's twin wing-tip tanks held a total capacity of 220 US-gallons which gave a range of 2000 miles, and 400lb of luggage could be stored in the former gun bays in the wings. Considering the aircraft's origins, a high degree of comfort was provided. The Cavalier's full instrument panel was arranged in vertical stacks and automatic heat controls were fitted to reduce the risk of overheating inherent in all liquid-cooled engines while taxying. For those already owning Mustangs a conversion kit was provided, and a choice of tanks allowed a variety of ranges. The late Ormond Haydon-Baillie flew a Cavalier at air displays in the United Kingdom in the 1970s but was killed when he crashed in Germany.

When it became apparent that the United States was likely to become involved in Southeast Asia in 1967, a counter-insurgency version of the Cavalier was proposed by the manufacturers. A 1760hp British Merlin 620 replaced the 1595hp Packard Merlin V-1650-7 of the Cavalier, but the Hamilton Standard four-bladed constant speed propeller was retained, as were the tip tanks. Provision was made for 4000lb of underwing stores and for six .5in Brownings. The P-51H type tail fin was fitted and an ejector seat was standard. The Mustang II was a two-seat version and the Turbo Mustang III, a private venture, carried a Rolls-Royce Dart 510 turboprop driving a Dowty-Rotol propeller in a very slender engine cowling. This version dispensed with the characteristic ventral radiator duct, and in clean configuration attained 540mph. In 1971 a new turbo version, the Enforcer, was produced by the renamed Cavalier Aircraft Corporation and had a 2535shp Lycoming T-55-L-9 turbine engine.

The United States Air Force adopted none of these designs. The Mustang now flies in peaceful skies, and its airworthiness nearly forty years after the first P-51 flew is a tribute to the design of a warplane which, by the very nature of its work, was not expected to last. While so many military aircraft were scrapped postwar, of which no examples remain, the Mustang is quite well represented. In the United States the Confederate Air Force still flies a number, including one F-82B, and when the USAF released its last ones in 1957, a P-51H (44-74936) of the West Virginia ANG was put on display at the Air Force Museum at Wright-Patterson Field. However only four P-51B and C examples appear to remain in the United States. An ex-RCAF P-51D is held at Duxford by the Imperial War Museum in the United Kingdom, appropriately in the markings of a machine flown by the 78th Fighter Group of the US 8th Air Force from that airdrome in the war and bearing the serial number 44-72258.

Right: **Cavalier Mustang II with six .5 caliber machine guns and six LAU-3/A rocket launchers with a total of 114 rocket projectiles. The aircraft was a company-financed project and was not taken up by the USAF.**

ANG
ANG

474850

N4222X

APPENDICES

1. Comparative data tables - Various marks of P-51

Engine	P-51A Allison V-1710-81	P-51B Packard Merlin V-1650-3	P-51D PM V-1650-7	P-51H PM V-1650-9	F-82G 2 × Allison V-1710-145
Horsepower	1,200	1,620	1,695	2,218	1,600 each
Wing span	37ft 0.25in	37ft 25in	37ft 0.25in	37ft	51ft 7in
Length	32ft 2.5in	32ft 3in	32ft 3.25in	33ft 4in	42ft 2.5in
Height	13ft 8in	13ft 8in	13ft 8in	13ft 8in	13ft 9.5in
Maximum speed (mph)	390 at 20,000ft	440 at 30,000ft	437 at 25,000ft	487 at 25,000ft	460 at 21,000ft
Maximum ceiling (ft)	31,350	42,000	41,900	41,600	28,300
Weight empty (lb)	6,433	6,840	7,125	6,585	15,997
Weight loaded (lb)	10,600	11,200	12,100	11,500	25,891
Range internal (miles)	750	550	950	755	2,240
Range drop tanks (miles)	2,350	2,200	2,080	1,530	4,000
Rate of climb (mins)	9.1 to 20,000ft	7 to 20,000ft	7.3 to 20,000ft	5 to 15,000ft	
Armament – guns	4 × 0.5in Browning	4 × 0.5in Browning	6 × 0.5in	6 × 0.5in	various
Armament – bombs/RP	2 × 500lb	2 × 1,000lb	or 6 × 5in RP		

2. Order of battle of USAAF 8th Air Force, UK, 1944

1st Air Division 67th Fighter Wing

Group	Squadrons	Identification	Cowling	Spinner	Tailplane	Base
20 FG	55 FS 77 FS 79 FS	KI LC MC	black and white vertical bars and spinner		black triangle black circle black square	Kingscliffe
352 FG	328 FS 486 FS 487 FS	PE P2 HO	blue	blue	red rudder yellow rudder blue rudder	Bodney
356 FG	359 FS 360 FS 361 FS	OC PI QI	red and blue checkers	red and blue checkers	yellow rudder red rudder, black bar blue rudder	Martlesham Heath
359 FG	368 FS 369 FS 370 FS	CV IV CS	green	green	yellow red blue	East Wretham
364 FG	383 FS 384 FS 385 FS	N2 5Y 5E	blue and white band behind spinner		black circle black square black triangle	Honington
364 Group Scouting Force		5E (9H wef March 1945)		red	red leading edges	

2nd Air Division 65th Fighter Wing

Group	Squadrons	Identification	Cowling	Spinner	Tailplane	Base
4 FG	334 FS 335 FS 336 FS	QP WD VF	red	red	red white blue	Debden/Steeple Morden
355 FG	354 FS 357 FS 358 FS	WR OS YF	red band behind white blue band behind white yellow band behind white		red blue yellow	Steeple Morden
361 FG	374 FS 375 FS 376 FS	B7 E2 E9	yellow	yellow	red blue yellow	Bottisham/Little Walden
479 FG	434 FS 435 FS 436 FS	L2 J2 9B	silver	silver	red yellow black	Wattisham
355 Group Scouting Force		WR	green and white cowling band		silver	

3rd Air Division 66th Fighter Wing

Group	Squadrons	Identification	Cowling and Spinner	Tailplane	Base
55 FG	38 FS	CG	green and yellow checkers and band	red	Wormingford
	338 FS	CL		green	
	343 FS	CY		yellow	
78 FG	82 FS	MX	black and white checkers	red	Duxford
	83 FS	WZ		black	
	84 FS	HL		white (edged red)	
339 FG	503 FS	D7	red and white checkered cowling	red	Fowlmere
	504 FS	5Q		green	
	505 FS	6N		yellow	
353 FG	350 FS	LH	yellow and black checkered cowling	yellow	Raydon
	351 FS	YJ		silver	
	352 FS	5X		black	
357 FG	362 FS	G4	red and yellow checkered band	silver	Leiston
	363 FS	B6		red	
	364 FS	C5		yellow	
55 Group Scouting Force		CL	green and yellow checkers and band	red and white checkers	
496 Fighter Training Group (555 FS)		C7			
7 Photographic Reconnaissance Group from January 1945				red rudder	

3. Order of Battle of other USAAF Air Forces

(listing component squadrons and identification letters where known)

Air Force	Group	Component Squadrons	Identification
5th	15 FG	78 FS	
	21 FG	45 FS	
		46 FS	
	506 FG	457 FS	
		485 FS	
9th	354 FG	353 FS	FT
	100 FW	355 FS	GQ
		356 FS	AJ
	363 FG	380 FS	A9
		381 FS	5M
		382 FS	C3
10th	311 FG	528 FS	
		529 FS	
		530 FS	
12th	52 FG		
14th	23 FG	74 FS	
	75 FS		
15th	31 FG	307 FS	M2
		308 FS	WZ
		309 FS	HL
	325 FG	317 FS	
		318 FS	
		319 FS	
	332 FG	99 FS	
		100 FS	
		301 FS	
		302 FS	

Bibliography

The Army Air Forces in WW2: Combat Chronology, Kit Carter and Robert Mueller, Office of Air Force History HQ USAF.
The Army Air Forces in World War II, edited by Wesley Craven and James Cate, University of Chicago Press.
World War II Fighter Conflict, Alfred Price, Macdonald and Jane's.
The Mighty Eighth, Roger Freeman, Military Book Society.
Airfields of the Eighth, Roger Freeman, After the Battle.
P-51 Bomber Escort, William Hess, Pan/Ballantyne.
Mustang at War, Roger Freeman, Ian Allan.
The North American Mustang, M J Hardy, David and Charles.
2nd TAF, Christopher Shores, Osprey.
The North American P-51B and C, Richard Atkins, Profile Publications.
Classic Aircraft – Fighters, Bill Gunston, Hamlyn.
Camouflages and Markings, James Goulding and Robert Jones, Doubleday & Co, NY

Acknowledgments

The author would like to thank the Taylor Picture Library for supplying the majority of the pictures for this book. The publisher would like to thank the following picture libraries and individuals for the following pictures:

Anglia Aeropics: pp 56 (bottom right), 57 (bottom left).
Bison Picture Library: p 41 (left).
Denis Hughes: pp 10–11 (top).
Imperial War Museum: pp 17 (top), 21 (bottom), 28 (top), 41 (right).
Martin and Kelman: pp 36–37.
North American: pp 4–5, 11 (center), 22–23, 25, 27, 28–29, 46–47, 52–53, 54–55.
Bob Snyder: pp 46 (below), 56 (bottom left), 57 (bottom left), 57 (top).
Taylor Picture Library: pp 14, 16.
USAF: pp 1, 2–3, 6–7, 8–9, 12, 13 (below), 18–19, 21 (top and center), 26 (inset), 30–31, 32, 35–36, 37, 38–39, 42–43, 44–45, 48–49, 50–51, 59 (top three), 60–61, 64.
US Army: pp 58–59.

Artwork

Mike Badrocke: Cutaway on pp 10–11, line drawing on p 13.
Mike Bailey: Cover sideview.
Mike Trim: Sideview on p 13.

Two Cavalier Mustangs leave Sarasota after being accepted by the USAF.